BRIGHTON & HOVE C

24 hour renewal service via

www.citylibraries.info

or tel: 0303 123 0035

To renew please have ready:

- Your library card number
- Your PIN for online, automated and self-service transactions

SAMUEL WALKER

© Copyright 2020 – All rights reserved.

The content contained within this book may not be reproduced, duplicated or transmitted without direct written permission from the author or the publisher.

Under no circumstances will any blame or legal responsibility be held against the publisher, or author, for any damages, reparation, or monetary loss due to the information contained within this book, either directly or indirectly.

Legal Notice:

This book is copyright protected. It is only for personal use. You cannot amend, distribute, sell, use, quote or paraphrase any part, or the content within this book, without the consent of the author or publisher.

Disclaimer Notice:

Please note the information contained within this document is for educational and entertainment purposes only. All effort has been executed to present accurate, up to date, reliable, complete information. No warranties of any kind are declared or implied. Readers acknowledge that the author is not engaged in the rendering of legal, financial, medical or professional advice. The content within this book has been derived from various sources. Please consult a licensed professional before attempting any techniques outlined in this book.

By reading this document, the reader agrees that under no circumstances is the author responsible for any losses, direct or indirect, that are incurred as a result of the use of the information contained within this document, including, but not limited to, errors, omissions, or inaccuracies.

Interior Design by FormattedBooks.com

TABLE OF CONTENTS

Introduction VII
    What it Takes.. VIII
        Who am I?.. X

Chapter 1: The Real Estate Utopia 1
    Myth #1 – My Home is the Best Investment 2
        Types of Returns 3
    Myth #2 – Real Estate is Safe 5
    Myth #3 – Real Estate Will Make You Rich… Fast! 8
    Myth #4 – I Need a Ton of Money to Invest! 11
    Myth #5 – I Need Specialized Knowledge 13
    Compounding 14

Chapter 2: The Pillars of Making Money 16
    Capital Appreciation 17
        Supply and Demand 18
        Inflation Rates 19
        Cost of Borrowing 19
        Market Forces 20
        What to be Wary of 21

Cash Flow 22
   Costs 24
   50% Rule 25
Tax Savings 26
   Ownership in a Self-Directed IRA 28
   Live in it for Two Years 29
   1031 Exchanges 29
   Never Sell 30

Chapter 3: Unique Characteristics of Real Estate 32
Residential 33
   Condominiums 34
   Manufactured Homes 35
   Modular Homes 36
   Multi Family 37
   Vacation Homes 37
   Single Family 38
   Town Houses 38
Office Buildings 39
   Income 40
   Relationships 41
   Limited Hours 42
   Price Evaluation 42
   Lease Structures 42
   Flexibility 43
   Disadvantages 43
   Ways to Invest 44
Shopping Centers 46
   Location and Traffic 47
   Age 48
   Tenant Quality 48
   Leases 49
   Competition 49
   REITs 50

Raw Land 51
Non-Traditional Investments 53

Chapter 4: Real Estate Versus Stocks 54
Investment Characteristics 55
Stock Investments 55
Physical Property Investing 58
Pros and Cons of Physical Real Estate 59
Advantages 59
Disadvantages 62
Pros and Cons of Investing in Stocks 65
Advantages 66
Disadvantages 67

Chapter 5: Get Your Hands Dirty 69
Strategy #1 – Plain Vanilla Rental Property 70
Property Type 70
Where to Invest 71
Finding Properties 73
Running Numbers 75
Strategy #2 – Fix and Flip 79
Offer Price 80
Financing 80
What to Look for 81
Calculating Profit 82
Strategy #3 – Vacation Rental Property 85
Strategy #4 – Foreclosure Investing 86

Chapter 6: Invest from Your Couch 89
REIT 90
The Easy Way 91
Analyzing Financials 94
Taxation 97
Investing in Real Estate Sector Stocks 98

Chapter 7: Key Rules of Thumb 99
    The One Percent Rule 100
        Drawbacks 101
    The 50% Rule 102
    The 70% Rule 103
    Cap Rates 105
    Dividend Yields 106

Chapter 8: Should I Quit My Job? 109
    The Early Days 110
        Network 111
        Financial Prep 112
    When to Quit 112

Conclusion 115

References 117

INTRODUCTION

"Games are won by players who focus on the playing field — not by those whose eyes are glued to the scoreboard."
– Warren Buffet

How does getting rich off real estate sound to you? This is something that almost everyone wants to achieve but the truth is that real estate isn't a get rich quick scheme. Although property is one of the most stable investments in America right now, this doesn't mean there aren't any risks associated with it.

The term 'real estate investor' by itself sounds intimidating. It conjures images of someone who has millions to invest and has a portfolio of entire apartment blocks and what not. However, the majority of real estate investors own single family homes that they lease to tenants. You too can be a successful real estate investor! It's just a matter of understanding how the game is played.

This book is going to give you deep insight into how you can go about making money off real estate. There are many strategies that you can implement and in here, you're going to learn about the pros and cons of all of them and you'll also be able to decide which method suits you best.

This is something that not enough investors take a note of. While every strategy will work in the long term, not every strategy can be implemented easily. Real estate investing strategies require differing levels of time commitment and financial resources. Depending on your situation, something that works well for 90% of people out there might just not be a good fit for you.

Many people run into such situations and think that they're just not cut out for real estate investing. This is nonsense! With the right strategy and proper planning, you will be able to cash in on the deals available around you.

WHAT IT TAKES

When people ask me what it takes to be successful at real estate, I often tell them that it's all a matter of getting organized. There are a lot of factors that you need to take into account and I'm going to show you each and every single one of them. They're not necessarily complicated. It's just that there are a decent number of them and a newbie might mistakenly think that all of this indicates that real estate is too complex for them.

Another hurdle that first time investors encounter is that they just don't have all the necessary information in place prior to investing in a property. All real estate deals involve financing of one kind or another. This means that you need to have all kinds of paperwork and proof ready to go and organized.

Lastly, as with any field of endeavor, there is a lot of jargon involved and you will need to understand what all of these terms mean. I'll be guiding you through all of these requirements so don't worry about this. The first place we'll begin is by taking a look at some myths that surround the topic.

Real estate investing is being practiced by so many people at the moment that this has led to all kinds of nonsense being peddled on the internet. You may have encountered some of these yourself and they might have fooled you into thinking something that just isn't true. Myth-busting is necessary before getting into the money-making pillars of real estate.

Most people think 'location, location, location' as being the only pillar of successful investing. This isn't the case. There's a lot more that goes on than just scouting a good location. In fact, you won't read the word location when I talk about these pillars! Before investing in anything, you need to understand what kinds of properties are available for you to invest in.

Residential real estate behaves very differently from commercial real estate. Further complicating things is the fact that you can have different sub-categories within these and they bring their own characteristics to the table. Getting to know all of them will help you figure out which type of property makes for the best investment for you.

Once all of this is done, we'll jump in and look at some extremely profitable investing strategies that you can employ. All of these strategies will be explained to you in layman's terms and truth be told, all of them are intuitive to a large extent. It's just that you need to learn the jargon associated with them in order to get started.

Something that will make your task a lot easier are simple rules of thumb that you can implement to quickly calculate whether an opportunity is worth your time or not. You won't need any calculators once you understand these simple rules. They'll shortcut your way to success for sure!

A common question that all successful real estate investors have to consider is whether they need to quit their jobs or not. This might sound like a good problem to have, but in reality, it is one that is fraught with danger. Making the wrong decision here might set you back by a lot and it is critical for you to evaluate your choices properly. I'll walk you through some of the things that I experienced in my journey to success and how you can learn from this.

Speaking of which, you might be wondering at this point who exactly Samuel Walker is? Well, allow me to introduce myself!

WHO AM I?

I am one of those people who can proudly call themselves a successful real estate investor. I didn't have any special resources at my disposal nor did I have any special talent for this field. When I first began, I can bet that I was even more clueless than you currently might be!

This is because there just weren't too many resources out there for new investors such as myself to learn the art of successful real estate investing. It wasn't as if I could just call a number or visit some website to figure out what to do next. My journey was slow and deliberate but eventually, I applied the strategies that made the most sense to me.

Funnily enough, I began investing in real estate through the stock market. My next stop was to invest in physical real estate and as my portfolio grew, so did the complexity of the deals I did. These days, I run a successful advisory firm for real estate investors and

I also own and manage a portfolio of residential and commercial properties within the United States.

When I tell beginners all of this, they tend to get intimidated and think that there must be some secret sauce to investing successfully in real estate. This simply isn't the case. All I've done is applied the principles I'm going to show you in this book and worked hard. That's really all there is to it. I've had some luck along the way as well, but so will you.

Real estate investing is often presented as being far more complex than it actually is. I'm here to show you that this isn't the case. If you want to make it complicated, you can certainly do so. However, you can be extremely successful by executing simple deals as well.

So, with all of this being said, let's now jump in and take a look at some myths surrounding real estate and let's see if you can spot a few that are holding you back!

CHAPTER 1
THE REAL ESTATE UTOPIA

Like with any endeavor that attracts a lot of money, real estate investing has its share of myths. Some of these myths originate from facts and this can make discerning between fact and fiction extremely tough. Then there are myths that push the theory that real estate investing is a cinch and that anyone can make money in it.

Well, this just isn't the case. You've perhaps had the unfortunate experience of having a deal go sour on you. Many people think that owning your own home and living in it means they're a real estate investor. This simply isn't the case as you'll learn.

Let's take a look at the biggest myths that are present in real estate and bust all of them, one by one!

MYTH #1 – MY HOME IS THE BEST INVESTMENT

This is the most common myth of them all and is often pushed with intelligent sounding maxims such as 'pay yourself before paying anyone else' and so on. Well, the fact is that real estate is a good investment. However, there is a severe lack of understanding amongst most people as to what an investment really is. This myth has emerged thanks to people not being able to figure out what an asset is and what a liability is.

Here's an example to help illustrate the difference: You're given an object, let's call it *A*, that costs you $100,000. You don't have the cash to pay for it and have to draw a loan to afford it. This means you'll need to pay interest and the real price you end up paying for *A* is $125,000. Once the deal is done and you've bought *A*, you cannot use it for anything else.

It sits there, much like a paperweight would, doing nothing. Is *A* an asset or a liability? Contrast this with another object *B*. *B* costs the same as *A* and is similar to *A* in every regard except one. *B* pays you a sum of $6000 per year as long as you hold onto it. Which object is the better investment: *A* or *B*?

Most people would say *B* in this case. Right after they say *B* is a good investment, they'll go out and apply for a mortgage to purchase a home with the intention of living in it. In other words, they'll say *B* is great and go out and buy something that behaves just as *A* does.

You might argue that a home provides you security and it appreciates in value. There's no doubt about the security aspect and I won't argue that. As for it appreciating in value, I'll address this in the second myth so let's leave it for now. However, understand that any investment needs to have two types of returns for it to qualify as an asset.

TYPES OF RETURNS

When you purchase a home, you can potentially earn two types of returns on it. The first is cash flow and the second is capital gains. When people mention that the price of a real estate investment rises over time, they're referring to capital gains. Capital gains are great and will always outstrip cash flow returns over time.

However, they're not guaranteed. Their existence depends on what the market does, and the markets are not guaranteed to rise. You'll learn more about this in the next myth. Assuming that the markets do rise, there's still another problem to deal with. Capital gains are unrealized for the most part.

When you own and live in a home the increase in its value is only on paper. Let's say your home's value appreciates by 10%. This is great! However, what can you do with that 10%? Can you withdraw it as cash? Can you increase your bank balance using this 10% gain? You can't do any of this.

You'll receive cash only if you sell your home. In other words, your gains are unrealized until you sell. Selling brings its own issues with it. While market rates indicate one thing, the true value of your investment is whatever a buyer is willing to pay for it. If the market veers into a ditch during the selling process, you're going to receive a lower price for it, no matter what average real estate values might be.

Cash flow returns on the other hand are realized gains. You can put this cash to work since it comes into your bank account. If you happen to buy a property and live in it, you're shutting off your cash flow returns and exposing yourself solely to capital gains returns. It might work out for you in the long run but there are no guarantees.

Cash flow on the other hand is real. If you rent a property out to a tenant, you're going to receive rental income every month. House hacking is an investment strategy whereby you live in your own property but still generate cash flow by renting out a portion of it to tenants. This is a great way to achieve the security of owning your own home and generating both kinds of returns on your investment.

Another aspect of home ownership that is overlooked by those who believe in this myth is that owning a home costs money. You need to pay property taxes and pay for regular maintenance. After all, every home suffers from a leaking pipe now and then. Over time, these expenses add up.

If your property was generating cash flow, which it won't if you choose to live in it solely, the cash you earn will pay for maintenance and you wouldn't be paying out of pocket. You don't need to wait till the day comes when you sell your home to earn back the cash that you spent maintaining the place; that is, if you earn capital gains when you sell.

So do not make the mistake of thinking that your home is a great investment by default. It is not an asset unless it's producing cash flow that you can lay your hands on. It's a liability if you're going to be relying on capital gains alone. Aim to build assets and understand that a property investment can turn into a liability depending on how you choose to deal with it.

MYTH #2 – REAL ESTATE IS SAFE

This myth has been sorely busted thanks to the housing crisis that occurred in 2008. However, there is a resurgence in it of late since people tend to have short memories. In fact, a lot of America has simply forgotten the crisis thanks to how painful it was. The years, or decades, leading up to the crisis were heady ones.

Homes in America kept rising in value, on paper, and there was a belief that housing prices would never crash. A justification for this phenomenon was that a home was an ordinary good and ordinary goods always rise in value in lockstep with inflation. Add to this fact that housing is something that will always be in demand and therefore this demand would ensure that appreciation rates would be higher than inflation.

I've thrown a few economic terms at you in that paragraph so let's define these before proceeding. The first is the term ordinary good. In economics, an ordinary good is something that is an everyday purchase or is something that people buy out of necessity. For example, groceries are ordinary goods. This is in contrast to luxury goods that are planned purchases and aren't necessary from a survival standpoint.

For example, do you really need a Ferrari to survive? You do need some form of conveyance though. Ordinary goods therefore increase in price slowly over time due to inflation while luxury goods' prices are driven solely by demand and supply and they're not subject to economic events. A Ferrari cost the same even when the market crashed in 2008 for example.

Inflation is an economic phenomenon where the prices of goods increase steadily over time. A loaf of bread used to cost 15 cents back in the 60s. It now costs around $3.00. Bread has become more expensive but the thing to keep in mind is that purchasing power has also increased.

The average income in the 60s was $4,007 per year (*Library Guides: Prices and Wages by Decade: 1960-1969*, 2020). These days it is $56,516. Inflation is a good thing since it means that demand for goods and services are increasing. As long as purchasing power increases in lockstep with it, this is good. However, stagnant purchasing power and increasing inflation is a bad thing.

This is what happened in the latter half of the previous decade. Demand for housing grew rapidly thanks to increased speculation in homes. Everyone thought that prices would rise forever and began borrowing money they couldn't afford. This in turn pushed prices even higher. A few lucky people managed to sell their overpriced homes and got out of the market.

The majority of people ended up being underwater on their mortgages. You're underwater on a mortgage when you owe more than what the property is worth. Runaway demand happens every now and then and causes problems. A lack of demand also causes problems.

If no one wants to buy homes, then prices will fall naturally. As of this writing, the world is experiencing a pandemic thanks to the spread of a virus. Unemployment rates are at an all-time high and are predicted to rival levels seen during the time of the Great Depression (*United States Initial Jobless Claims 2021-2022 Forecast*, 2020).

How will people be able to afford homes? More importantly, how will they pay for their current home when they don't have sustainable employment? All of this will create a fall in housing values. Having said that, it also represents an opportunity for the savvy investor to buy undervalued assets.

My point is that the real estate market fluctuates just as the stock market does. Assuming that the market is safe just because real estate involves a solid asset such as a home is a mistake. The real estate market fluctuates according to its own whims and you are exposed to it when you purchase real estate. This is why it's important to generate cash flow from your investment and not rely on just capital gains.

Something that makes the real estate market slightly riskier than the stock market is that there is a lot of leverage tied to it. Leverage refers to when people borrow money to pay for things. Mortgages are a form of leverage. While leverage increases your cash on cash gains, it can also increase your losses.

Let's say you borrow $150,000 (you pay $50,000 of your own money) to purchase a $200,000 property. If you manage to spruce it up and rehab it, its market value increases to $250,000. This means that your cash on cash gain is 100%. You invested $50,000 of your own cash and the property appreciated by $50,000. This is a 100% gain.

Let's say the market crashes and the value of the property decreases to $150,000. In this scenario, you've just lost 100%. Leverage cuts both ways and accelerates your profit and loss equally. It is also possible to lose more than your initial investment amount. This is what causes real estate crashes to accelerate since leverage fuels almost all transactions.

All in all, keep in mind that while the real estate market represents opportunity, it also represents risk. Carefully managing risk is the key to success.

MYTH #3 – REAL ESTATE WILL MAKE YOU RICH... FAST!

You may have heard of the fixer and flipper who made $50,000 over the course of three months or some investor who bought a foreclosure and realized a $100,000 profit in the matter of a month. These happen to be exceptional results and are far from the norm. The normal state of real estate investing is a lot more boring than this.

Over the past century, studies indicate that the real estate market appreciates at an average rate of seven percent per year (Davis, 2020). This is almost equal to the appreciation rate that the stock market witnesses.

Such decidedly unsexy returns are what you can expect over the lifetime of your real estate investment. Note, I'm not saying that you will realize these returns. It's just that this is the average, so harboring notions of getting rich quickly or overnight is unrealistic. Instead it is far better to focus on playing the game well instead of looking at the scoreboard.

There are many real estate strategies that you can use to increase your wealth. Strategies such as BRRRR, house hacking, fixing and flipping, buying foreclosures, real estate wholesaling and so on offer the prospect of large returns. The problem is that you need expertise and patience to make these work. You also need a dash of luck to be able to realize outsized profits.

Many investors jump into these strategies and don't take into account the amount of work and preparation that needs to be done prior to executing them. Much like how they believe that the real estate market is guaranteed to be safe, they equally believe that employing a strategy is an automatic guarantee of riches.

Well, this simply isn't the case. It is possible to lose money when utilizing these strategies if you're not careful and prepared. The most important time to determine whether you'll make money is before you jump into a strategy and move ahead with it. The presence of leverage can destroy your net worth if you're not careful.

A good practice to carry out is to build a margin of safety in every aspect of your investment. I'd say that it's best to employ this in all areas of your life but this isn't a book about personal finance. Instead, I'll stick to just real estate. When estimating the profitability of a project and taking costs into account, overestimating costs and underestimating returns will help you take unforeseen events into account better.

Adding a line item in your cost analysis labelled 'miscellaneous' is another way of building a margin of safety into your investment. These sound like small things but they'll save you money in the long run. The fact is that there are many unforeseen risks you run when employing real estate investment strategies.

Let's say you located a property to fix and flip. You lined up the mortgage and contractors and everything was set to go until the lock down measures began. Now, you're the proud owner of a decrepit property that is rotting every single day it stands. Your mortgage needs to be paid out of pocket for six months now instead of three thanks to the delay that the lockdown will cause.

This puts additional strain on your finances which were at the limit as it is. Worse, your spouse or partner just announced that they've been laid off. The stimulus check of $1,200 that you're going to receive sure will help a lot! Just kidding, it's not going to do anything to help you clear your loan.

While this is an exaggeration for the most part, the fact is that current global events demonstrate how this is possible. There are many people in this exact situation right now and those who have built a margin of safety into their investment metrics will survive. Those who haven't will be buried in debt.

So don't assume that real estate is a get rich quick scheme. Do your homework and always build a margin of safety.

MYTH #4 – I NEED A TON OF MONEY TO INVEST!

I've been indulging in doom and gloom over the past two myths so it's now time for some good news. The short version: You don't need a lot of money to invest in real estate successfully. Let's look at this in more detail since it's not as if you don't need any money at all to successfully invest.

Most real estate investors use leverage as you've already learned. This is done by securing mortgages from lending institutions. There are a large number of institutions in the United States that offer loans to investors when it comes to real estate investment. In fact, the government operates one of the largest home loan programs in the country under the umbrella of the Federal Housing Authority (FHA).

FHA loans offer buyers a number of truly attractive terms and best of all, they offer loans to people with less than perfect credit as well. The point here is that it is not all that difficult to qualify for a mortgage even if your bank denies your application.

The only people who buy homes in cash are the super rich who do it for wealth preservation and tax purposes. As such, their aim isn't wealth generation so these cases aren't really applicable to you. The biggest expenses you will encounter are down payment and closing costs.

These can run into the low five figures on most mortgages. While this might be a bit too high for you to afford, this doesn't mean you cannot invest in real estate. For starters, there are many ways to receive down payment assistance. There are a large number of federal down payment assistance programs you can use.

In addition to this, you can source your down payment from family and friends as well. If these are not viable options for you, you can still invest in real estate through the stock market. This is how I started out in fact. You can invest in companies that are involved in the real estate market or you can invest in companies that manage properties. The latter stocks are called real estate investment trusts and you'll learn all about them later in this book.

You can invest in the stock market with as little as $100. So let go of the notion that you need tons of cash to make this work. Another myth that people believe is that you need to have a lot of cash to support ongoing costs. Let's use house hacking as an example to prove how wrong this is.

With house hacking, investors purchase a property and place a portion of it on lease. They live in the property and thus pay their mortgage. However, the rental payment that they earn goes a long way towards decreasing their mortgage and maintenance costs. In some markets, the rental income actually matches the mortgage payment and thus, they get to live in their home for free!

Often, real estate investments will generate excess cash and this will allow you to build a good slush fund for emergencies. A good rule of thumb to follow here is to maintain six months' worth of expenses in the bank. Some investors tend to get greedy and over leverage themselves.

This is partly where this myth comes from. People on the outside see the investor struggling to make cash payments and conclude that the investment requires a ton of cash. In reality, what's happened here is that the investor has taken on too much leverage. As Warren Buffet has mentioned in one of his letters to the shareholders of his company, he would rather forego an interesting opportunity rather than over leverage his balance sheet.

Successful real estate investment requires you to balance your levels of debt and equity. Manage these well and you'll find that real estate investing will generate great returns for you and you won't find yourself needing huge amounts of cash. If you don't have a ton of cash, focus on investing whatever you can in the stock market regularly.

Even if the amount is small, this will allow you to earn some income on your investment and you'll have the twin engines of cash flow and capital gains working for you.

MYTH #5 – I NEED SPECIALIZED KNOWLEDGE

Can you add? Can you subtract, multiple and divide? Can you rein in your mind when it tries to run away with unbridled optimism thinking that you're going to make millions overnight?

If you can do these things, you have everything you need to succeed at real estate investing. A lot of beginners think that they need a degree in construction or some special license to be able to succeed. They look at the real estate agent world and notice that almost everyone is a smooth talker and is an aggressive personality. They think that they can't really compete with this and sit aside.

The fact is that being an investor and being an agent are two different things entirely. An agent's job is to sell. You're here to make money. The two aren't connected. Sure, you will need to network with people but it's not as if you need to know everyone under the sun or pound the pavement trying to generate sales.

Marketing efforts are necessary mainly to help you find tenants. You will need to build a small network of agents and contractors that can help you with any maintenance or rehab work that you need carried out. The entire investing process sounds complex from the outside looking in but the fact is that you will be guided every step of the way by an agent or by the relevant authorities.

Your responsibility is to simply be realistic about the project and to estimate returns in a logical manner. As long as you don't project your pie in the sky wishes onto what professionals are telling you, you'll be just fine. With regards to legalities, real estate investing is practiced by so many newbies that there is an entire support system dedicated to helping you navigate the process.

You don't need to worry about setting up escrow accounts or conducting inspections and all of this. You will need to be aware of what these entail, of course, but don't think that this is a large scale project that you need to manage personally. Neither do you need to hire employees or manage different personalities.

Real estate investing is a simple process that is complicated by wishful thinking. Avoid this and you'll be more than successful.

COMPOUNDING

As a final word, I'd like to introduce you to the concept of compounding. You'll probably be familiar with it but many people understand it intellectually and neglect the implications of it in reality. Your biggest gains are going to come via the power of compounding.

A dollar invested in the broad stock market in 1969 will be worth $19.69 today. That's what happens when an average gain of 7% compounds over time. When it comes to real estate investing, you need to remain invested for a long period of time. This is when the cash flows from your property will add up and your capital gains will also increase since you'll be giving your investment more time to appreciate.

What most investors who fail tend to do is to give into the short term fluctuations of the market and sell during market bottoms. They read that the housing market is collapsing and they want to get out before it gets worse. They might also think that maintaining a property is a headache and that it just isn't worth it and they'll look to sell.

All of this is an example of how emotions cloud your judgment. Keep these away when it comes to investing and always remind yourself of the power of compounding. The longer you stay invested, the greater your gains will be.

CHAPTER 2
THE PILLARS OF MAKING MONEY

The three pillars of making money in real estate are cash flows, tax savings and capital appreciation. Depending on your investment strategy, the relative importance of these three factors will fluctuate. However, they'll always show up regardless of which strategy you employ.

This chapter is going to educate you on how they work and what you can do to ensure that all three pillars are always by your side.

CAPITAL APPRECIATION

Capital appreciation is what creates capital gains. This is when your property's value increases over time. You buy a property for $250,000 and it increases in value to $400,000. That's capital appreciation. A significant thing to take into account when looking at capital appreciation is the amount of time it takes to appreciate.

If your property increased by that amount in a year, then that's a huge gain. If it takes 50 years to appreciate that much, then it's worse than a savings account. In other words, you'd have been better off placing that money in a regular savings account that pays one percent interest per year.

As I detailed in the previous chapter, many investors enter the market looking at just the appreciation factor. They don't take into account the other costs of ownership and shut off their cash flow by deciding to live in the place. The thing with capital appreciation is that you have no way of knowing what the rate of appreciation is going to be.

Many investors new to the game buy property in cities such as New York or San Francisco thinking that demand will be ever-present in these cities and with space at a premium, this means that property prices will always appreciate. The national media also contributes to this feeling by breathlessly reporting how prices in these cities rose by 10% or 20%.

Well, the fact is that figuring out capital appreciation is a bit more complex than this. Here are the factors that determine the rate at which your property will increase in value.

SUPPLY AND DEMAND

This one is rather obvious and is just basic economics really. The greater the demand and shorter the supply, the more prices will increase. What most people ignore is the type of demand when speaking of this equation. Let's take New York City for example and more specifically, Manhattan.

The type of demand that the borough witnesses is definitely on the higher end of the scale. An average renter in Manhattan pays $4,208 for their apartment (*Average Rent in Manhattan & Rent Prices by Neighborhood*, 2020). Paying $1,500 a month will get you an apartment in a terrible neighborhood where security and facilities will be an issue.

The average cost of property is pretty high in Manhattan and this means that demand is skewed between to extremes. On one hand, you have people who cannot afford to buy an apartment and are looking to rent. On the other hand, you have ultra wealthy people who can afford places and are looking to buy property for their own living purposes or are looking to rent them out.

This creates odd demand curves. Typically, high-end user demand (where buyers live in the place themselves) creates high capital appreciation. However, given that there are a large number of rental seekers as well, this tends to dampen appreciation rates. This is why the rates of appreciation in big cities tend to be all over the place and inconsistent.

This is despite demand being high. So always keep the quality of demand at the top of your mind when investing.

INFLATION RATES

As I described earlier, housing is a common good and as such you can expect appreciation rates to match inflation rates at the very least over the long term. Over the short term, appreciation rates will track sentiment and will vary. Keep in mind that if your property is appreciating at just the inflation rate, then you're essentially standing still in terms of what your money is worth.

A dollar today is worth $1.02 a year from now as per current inflation statistics in the United States. Another way of looking at this is that you'll need to pay $1.02 a year from now for all the stuff you can buy for a dollar today. If inflation is all you're going to earn from your property, then you're better off placing your money elsewhere.

COST OF BORROWING

The real estate market depends a lot on interest rates. When interest rates increase, the cost of borrowing increases and thus the demand for homes decreases. When this happens, prices fall. Truth be told, there is nothing you can do to control this factor. It's best to simply be aware of this and not try to predict which way interest rates will move.

After all, if you can't predict interest rate movements successfully (which almost no one can), you're better off day trading your money!

MARKET FORCES

There are many drives that affect property values. Development of additional property such as offices, hospitals and other facilities boost values. The construction of a road that connects the property to a main center of the city also boosts values. Population growth also affects property values.

In addition to this, zoning regulations that suppress supply by enforcing the creation of green spaces also tend to boost property values. There are some factors you can predict or analyze here but again, over the long run, there isn't much you can do to control any of them.

All in all, capital appreciation is a matter of the stars aligning for you. You can expect property values to appreciate over the long term but your ability to earn greater than average market returns comes down to special circumstances. There are ways to force property appreciation of course.

You can carry out improvements to it and make it a better place to live. You can reduce your expenses running that place and this will boost your returns from it. However, none of these methods can deliver outsized gains and are in fact steps you should take as a matter of routine.

The best way to realize large appreciation rates is by choosing strategies that target them. For example, buying foreclosures or fixing and flipping are two strategies that create huge capital gains.

Both strategies have their risks of course, but if appreciation is your primary goal then you should focus on executing these.

Keep in mind that proper estimation of costs and expenses is the key to making these work. You'll learn all about this later in the book. For now, keep in mind everything you've learned and understand that targeting just capital appreciation is a bad strategy unless you're implementing the methods highlighted.

WHAT TO BE WARY OF

A particular thing to be wary of when it comes to capital appreciation potential is media hype. This often happens in the bigger cities where you'll read about how property prices jumped by double digits for three years and so on. As I mentioned earlier, the quality of demand in these places means that appreciation rates are all over the place.

What you will not read about is how growth rates remain flat for a long period of time and prices will go nowhere. This means you'll see growth of 10% for three years and then zero for 10 years. This is precisely what happens in markets such as Honolulu and San Francisco.

Everyone wants that special house overlooking the bay or the beach but they don't take into account the fact that inflated prices rarely tend to appreciate. What's more, these properties do not command high levels of rent and as a result, they don't make for great rental property investments either (Carson, Lewis, & Olivier, 2019).

There's a reason why only the ultra-wealthy purchase property in these places. It's because stable property rates mean that they're great places to park money in and ensure that money will grow at the rate of inflation at the very least. So, keep all of this in mind when you feel the need to invest in property solely for the purpose of capturing capital appreciation.

Again, I'm not saying that this is a bad approach. It's just that you need to execute the appropriate strategies that will bring about this result in the best way possible.

CASH FLOW

Many newbie investors, be they real estate or stock market investors, grossly underestimate how important cash flow is. Cash is what drives business and is what enables you to go out and enjoy the fruits of your success. For example, let's say you have $1 million sitting in a brokerage account as unrealized gains but you've just lost your job.

Let's further assume that you can't withdraw that capital for whatever reason. Is that million going to do you any good? Likely not! It isn't cash and you're not going to be able to spend it on anything. The most important aspect of cash flow, aside from using it to pay your bills, is that it provides free leverage to grow your wealth.

What do I mean by this? I've just spent an entire chapter telling you how leverage can cut both ways and have warned you about it. Does this mean cash flow cuts both ways as well? Not quite. You see, a high level of cash flow is free leverage. In other words, you don't need to pay anyone interest when you utilize cash flow to power your investments.

Let's look at this via an example. Let's say you have $100,000 to invest and decide to buy an asset that generates $1000 in cash every month. That's $12,000 you'll receive in cash by the end of the year.

Now, let's say you reinvest that $12,000 into an asset that generates $100 every month. This brings in $1,200 every year.

You invest that $1,200 into a third asset that generates $50 every month which brings in $600 per year. Let's take stock of what your cash returns look like at this point, before capital gains.

Your initial investment is $100,000. This has generated $36,000 over three years. You've invested $24,000 of this money to earn a further $3,600 over two years. At the end of the third year, you've received $600 from your third investment. The reinvestments that you carried out came from existing cash flows and you didn't have to invest any additional amount of money.

Therefore, your total investment stands at $100,000 while your overall gains are $40,200. This is a gain of 40.2% over three years and that's just from cash flow. If your investments increase in terms of capital appreciation, your investment has grown further.

Does this example sound farfetched to you? Well, it's actually very similar to what Warren Buffett did back in the 1960's and continues to do this day, albeit these days he operates on a far bigger scale. Buffett didn't execute this plan in the real estate market. Instead, his market of choice was the stock market. However, his methods hold a lot of lessons for savvy real estate investors.

By buying businesses that produced tons of cash, Buffett was able to redirect the cash that was earned in even more investments that earned cash. He bought insurance businesses and newspapers which were huge cash cows back then. For a real estate investor, the way forward is clear and echoes what you learned in the previous chapter.

Cash flow is what truly powers your investment and allows you to supercharge your returns. While cash flow from a single property will be lesser than the capital gains you can potentially earn from it, the true power of cash happens when you invest it into another place and generate cash and capital gains from the second investment.

In effect, your first investment is paying for your second and this is the free leverage I was talking about. Without borrowing a cent or even doing anything extra, you get to increase the value of your investment portfolio. Some ways of increasing cash flow in your rental properties is to justify the charging of higher rent.

Investing to spruce up the property, installing new appliances and making the bathrooms more attractive are all examples of things you can do to justify higher rent. These days many people live with pets. There are two ways you can approach this. The first is the traditional way whereby you charge fees for the pets.

The new, and more sustainable, way would be to open your property to pets and to charge a higher rent. Psychologically, people will be more willing to pay higher rents than pay a 'fee' per month. You will have to spend more on maintenance but the higher quality of life your tenants have will justify this policy.

COSTS

Speaking of maintenance, an area that investors often get wrong is with regards to estimating cash flow from their prospective investments. The free cash flow from your property is the rental payments minus any repairs, maintenance and even utilities. While electricity and gas are usually paid for by the tenant, water and sewage can be paid by the landlord or tenant.

If your property happens to be in a community, you might have to pay common area maintenance or other neighborhood related maintenance fees. Lastly, you must also keep in mind that your mortgage payment is an expense and you need to factor this into your costs.

Depending on your market, you can conceivably have your mortgage paid for by the rent you earn. This isn't always possible but it's a good goal to shoot for, nonetheless. When evaluating the profitability of an investment, a good rule of thumb to use is to see if you can earn one percent of the total acquisition cost as rent.

For example, if the cost of the property is $100,000 and you spent another $10,000 rehabbing the place, your total acquisition cost is $110,000. One percent of this is $1100. If you can earn this much in rent per month, the property deserves a deeper look.

This rule will help you out of a jam especially when it comes to properties in major cities. For example, if you decide to purchase a million-dollar property in San Francisco, you're going to have to earn $10,000 in rent per month! The average rent in that city is $4,000 so this makes the property a pretty bad investment.

50% RULE

Another rule of thumb to use when estimating costs is to divide your rental income by half and to assume that this is how much you'll pay as expenses to maintain and run the property. This is a neat way to also take into account non-cash expenses and intermittent expenses on your property.

The difficult part for most beginner investors is to get their heads around how they need to account for maintenance expenses. These don't occur every single month and when they do occur, they tend to leave a hold in your pocket. Then there's the degree of maintenance that needs to be carried out.

Some months you might need to ensure the lawn is mowed but other months, you might need to replace the entire roof within a few days in order to ensure the house is livable. This is why setting aside half of your rental cash flow for expenses is a good strategy.

This also helps you calculate your cap rate which is a metric you'll learn about in more detail later. The cap rate is calculated by dividing the total expenses by the acquisition cost. In other words, it's the return you receive on your investment.

All in all, the point here for you to take away is that you need to focus a lot more on your cash flow than on the capital appreciation. While both are important, cash flow is what turbocharges your investment returns by giving you access to free leverage.

TAX SAVINGS

When it comes to any investment, let alone real estate investing, minimizing your cost of investing is crucial. Taxes and transaction costs eat up a lot of your gains and can make a huge difference to your bottom line. While minimizing taxes is important, some investors get carried away and get a little too creative when it comes to this.

The net result is that they end up spending more on maintaining the structure that they've created than the amount they would have paid as taxes. When it comes to investing in the stock market, transaction costs are typically low but they add up to quite a lot over time and depend on how often you trade.

Brokers charge commissions for every trade you place and while the commission on a single trade is low, if you invest every single month, these costs will add up to quite a lot. The best option is to choose a broker that offers zero commission accounts or an app that lets you invest for free. For example, Robinhood is an app that allows you to invest for free and Charles Schwab is a full-service broker that offers zero commission accounts.

Investing for the long term is something that you must do to avoid increasing both your transaction costs as well as taxes. While a zero-commission broker won't charge you anything for holding onto your investments for a short while, the government will charge you a higher tax rate if you sell your investment within a year.

The IRS states that all investments sold within a year have their gains taxed at the ordinary income rate. Those that are held onto for longer than a year will be taxed at the capital gains taxes rate. Capital gains taxes range from zero to 20% and depend on your filing status. However, no matter your income bracket and filing status, the capital gains tax rate is lower than the ordinary income tax rate.

Holding onto your investments for the long term also allows you to give them time to mature and grow in size. It also makes it easy to manage your investment portfolio. After all, you simply buy and hold for as long as possible. Many investors fall prey to emotions in the market and think that everything's going to come crashing down the minute the markets turn downwards. For example, the current health crisis has caused huge sellers in the market.

While some degree of selling is warranted, does it really justify some of the valuations that are being implied for multi-billion-dollar companies? Don't let your emotions ruin your investment. Instead, stay invested for the long term and let compounding work its magic.

The same applies to brick and mortar real estate as well. Thankfully, selling physical real estate is a lengthy process and this prevents people from selling at the drop of a hat. One of the advantages of investing in physical real estate is that you can significantly lower your tax bill by claiming a number of benefits.

There are a number of expenses you can deduct from your taxes such as (Brumer-Smith, 2020):
- Property taxes
- Mortgage interest
- Property repairs
- Advertising expenses (to source tenants)

Then there's depreciation expense. The idea is that your property faces wear and tear over time and this creates a non-cash expense. The IRS allows you to deduct a specific amount every year and this reduces your tax bill. Maximizing deductions and depreciation are the most effective ways of reducing taxes on your investment.

There are other methods as well and let's take a look at these.

OWNERSHIP IN A SELF-DIRECTED IRA

A self-directed IRA is a slightly complicated legal structure but if used in the right way, it can reduce your tax bills significantly. This isn't as straightforward as owning stocks in an IRA portfolio. Here, you will need to approach a custodian and have them set up an IRA for you.

You will need to set up an LLC that will own your properties. This allows you to defer taxes on the property until you retire, much like with an IRA. There are a few downsides to this you need to be aware of. The first is that getting financing for such legal entities is tough.

What I mean is that if you wish to finance a property through your LLC in the IRA, you'll have a hard time finding lenders willing to finance you. This is because the financing within these structures tends to be what is called non-recourse. This means the lender cannot hold you personally liable for the funds in case of default. As you can imagine this is a problem for most lenders.

However, this doesn't mean it's impossible to invest in this way. The best way forward is to speak to a custodian and a CPA and see if this solution makes sense for you.

LIVE IN IT FOR TWO YEARS

Some people actually use this as a full-fledged investment strategy. It's called a live in flip. An investor locates a home requiring upgrades or rehab work, finances it and fixes it up. They live in it for a period of two years and then sell it. From a tax standpoint, the first $250,000 for singles and $500,000 for married couples is tax free.

These amounts typically mean that the capital gains earned on a flip become completely tax free. While it isn't a long-term strategy for most people, those starting out investing in real estate will receive a nice capital boost by utilizing this strategy.

1031 EXCHANGES

Also called like-for-like exchanges, in this method you exchange your property for another one just like it. This way you get to buy another property and defer taxes on your first purchase. Here's how it works. Let's say you earn a $30,000 profit on your first deal.

Instead of keeping it as cash in your account, you invest that profit as a down payment for another property within the tax year. The new property could be even more valuable. and you could earn a bigger profit from it. By performing another 1031 exchange within the tax year, you get to defer taxes in this way until you decide to stop doing this and own no more real estate.

So how long can you keep doing this for? Indefinitely as per current IRS rules. In fact, that brings me to my next point.

NEVER SELL

That's right! If you never sell your property, you'll never pay capital gains taxes on it. Keep earning rental income and pass it on to your heirs. Here's the great part about this. When you die, the cost basis of the home (that is the effective purchase price) resets to the value of the home during the day of your passing.

Your heirs therefore do not need to pay any taxes on the property they inherit and get to keep enjoying the rental income they earn from the place. A similar advantage is available when investing in REITs as well (real estate investment trusts that I mentioned previously).

REITs pay dividends to their investors and if you hold on forever, portions of those dividend payments reduce your effective purchase price as per IRS rules. Over time, your effective purchase price could dive to zero and you can pass this onto your heirs without paying taxes.

This brings to a close our look at the pillars of making money in real estate. Don't get caught up in the exact ways you can execute all of these. At this point, what you need to focus on is the fact that these three pillars need to become your mindset when it comes to real estate investing.

Understand how capital appreciation works, focus on cash flow and minimize taxes. Your rate of return will take care of itself. Depending on your strategy, one factor might be more important than another but at the end of the day, all of them will be present in one form or another.

CHAPTER 3
UNIQUE CHARACTERISTICS OF REAL ESTATE

There are many types of properties you can invest in. The type of property you choose dictates your investment experience since each category behaves differently. There are five categories of real estate you can buy. This chapter is going to outline their characteristics and you can accordingly choose which one appeals to you the most.

Keep in mind that there is no 'best' or 'worst' category. It all comes down to your outlook and how you choose to view risk.

RESIDENTIAL

This is the most highly advertised and crowded category of real estate investment. Mind you, crowded doesn't mean bad. In fact, the crowd is an advantage because information transparency is high and there are dedicated support networks to help investors at every stage of the process.

There are different kinds of residential real estate you can purchase. Here they are in no order of preference:
- Condominiums
  - Condotels
- Manufactured homes
- Modular homes
- Multi family
- Vacation homes
- Single family
- Townhouses

CONDOMINIUMS

Also called condos, these are often confused with apartments. Physically, condos and apartments look the same and even cost the same. However, there are a number of subtle differences that make them very different.

The first difference is with regards to ownership. An apartment is a part of a building that has a single owner. The owner usually delegates property management to another company that collects rent, maintains the place and so on. You pay your rent to this company and liaise with them in case of any issues or questions.

A condo complex on the other hand can have multiple owners owning the units within. On a single floor, you can have as many owners as there are units. The place is maintained by the homeowners' association and not by a company. This gives rise to a few costs that you would not have in the case of an apartment.

The association will charge you fees and you might have to agree to a few other rules that they impose. While apartment rules tend to be a standard set, a few condos can have quirky rules. For example, you might not be allowed to rent the place on Airbnb as a vacation home.

Understanding these rules is important prior to purchasing a unit. There may also be a few differences when it comes to the way utilities are handled. Most apartment complexes include utilities in the rent but condos typically break them out. You can pass these on to your tenant but you should still be aware of how utility payments work.

A subset of condominiums are condotels which are serviced apartments that you can buy within a complex. There will be a reception desk and a concierge along with all kinds of facilities such as a gym or a sauna available to residents. These are typically aimed at short term and vacation renters and mortgage lenders consider them a hybrid of commercial and residential real estate. Therefore, you'll find it tough to get approved for financing when it comes to these.

MANUFACTURED HOMES

These used to be called mobile homes or trailers and typically they're placed on leased land. The home itself is built on top of a non-removable steel chassis and hitches onto the back of a truck or any other vehicle. They've long been associated with low income housing, but these days have become a lifestyle of choice for many retirees.

There are a few pros to investing in these. The first is that thanks to their pre-fabricated nature, they can be built and installed quickly. All materials that go into these homes are manufactured in Housing and Urban Development (HUD) approved factories and as a result, their quality can be as high, if not higher, than regular homes.

Utility bills also tend to be low with these homes thanks to their energy efficient nature. The lack of complicated materials in these homes also means that there's less risk associated with building them. For example, you won't need to worry about copper pipes and wires being stolen.

The downside is that they're viewed as alternative investments despite being residential real estate. Their non-traditional nature, and stigma about being suited for low income housing, means that lenders turn the other way when you approach them regarding financing.

Their design also tends to adopt a one size fits all approach since there's only so much variation one can achieve with prefabricated parts. The stigma surrounding them means that their appreciation value can be low when compared to regular homes.

Lastly, a huge hurdle when it comes to investing in these is that land in crowded metropolitan areas is expensive and most of the time, you'll find it hard to receive approval to park a home on them. A lot of land leases stipulate that any construction that takes place needs to be permanent and this rules out mobile homes of all kinds.

However, in the right place and with the right financing, these homes make for good investments.

MODULAR HOMES

Thanks to the stigma surrounding mobile homes, modular homes came into existence. These don't have the trailer-like look but are prefabricated homes. They don't hitch onto the back of a truck or have wheels but are instead transported on the back of a flatbed. These homes resemble an on-site-built home and come with the same bells and whistles.

In other words, it is possible for them to have a basement and crawl space and so on. The advantage is that they can be built a lot faster since they use prefabricated parts. They're also far more energy efficient than site-built homes.

The standard of design is quite high and the financing options available on them are pretty similar to site-built homes. They're a good choice if you wish to consider single family homes.

MULTI FAMILY

These properties have multiple units in them, hence the name. For example, a block of four apartments is a multi-family property. They're also referred to as multi units in common parlance. Multi-family units are the preferred choice for house hackers and many rehabbers also find that these provide huge gains once they're refurbished.

Multi-family units are a popular investment and for this reason, you will find that financing on them follows traditional lines. You won't need to worry about anything outside of what is typically asked of borrowers. Multi-family housing works very well with almost every investment strategy.

Despite this, there are some that are better suited for this type of property than others. For example, fixing and flipping is theoretically possible but this depends on the number of repairs that need to be carried out. If the repairs are too much, you might find that the extent of them makes the project unviable.

As I mentioned earlier, house hacking is a great strategy to deploy with these properties. This is because the investor can live in one unit while renting out the others. It provides everyone with their own living space and makes the experience all the better.

VACATION HOMES

These properties can be condos, single family homes and even multi-units. The reason they get tagged with the vacation label is due to the fact that they're often found near or in spots that are vacation destinations. They're typically monetized by renting them out on sites like Airbnb.

Alternatively, they also function as a wealth maintenance vehicle for the rich. Chalets and lodges in ski towns, beachfront property in the islands etc., all serve this purpose. Monetization isn't the primary goal with them. Following the one percent rule will help you avoid sinking money into a property that is better suited for wealth maintenance as opposed to wealth generation.

SINGLE FAMILY

These are the most common forms of homes found in the United States. Think of the average home in suburbia. This is what a single-family home looks like. It could have any number of bedrooms and bathrooms and typically comes with some sort of yard out in front.

These properties are perfect for fixing and flipping and usually generate great returns. Even plain vanilla rental income investing works very well with these properties. Tenants tend to be families so you can expect some level of stability in terms of rental income.

House hackers can choose these kinds of properties but the downside is that they'll be effectively leasing out bedrooms and basements. This means that they'll have to share the common areas with different people and privacy could be a concern. However, a lot of people make this work very well for them.

TOWN HOUSES

These are a type of single-family units where additional units are attached to the side instead of being part of the same structure or above and below as is the case with a condo. Town houses are usually found in bigger cities and thanks to being treated as single-family residences, they receive the same financing benefits as regular single-family homes.

The categories mentioned above can apply at the same time to a single property. As such, they're not mutually exclusive. Whatever the type of property you're investing, the investment principles for you to abide by are the same. Make sure you follow the steps indicated in the strategies listed in this book and evaluate profits using the rules of thumb you'll learn about later.

Categorizing a property is a good way for you to quickly understand what sort of a strategy you're best off following. Don't get too carried away with the categories despite this. Remember, your returns are what matter the most so focus on this above all else.

OFFICE BUILDINGS

Office buildings fall firmly into the category of commercial real estate. Commercial real estate tends to be more volatile than residential. This is because as business conditions sour, tenants tend to move quickly and it can be hard to renew leases. Unlike families that always need a roof over their heads, companies can choose to shift their operations online during tough times or lease less expensive office space temporarily.

Having said that, when times are good, commercial real estate tends to boom. Tenants are typically high quality given that they're businesses and you can enforce rules and rent increases in a more orderly fashion with them. An office building can include the following types of property:

1. Retail outlets
2. Commercial offices
3. Mixed use buildings (residential and commercial)
4. Hotels
5. Warehouses

Each of these have their own subtleties but they tend to follow similar lines of thought when it comes to investment principles. There are many advantages when it comes to investing in office buildings so let's take a look at these.

INCOME

The rental yield on office buildings is typically a lot more than residential real estate. While residential rental yields (rental payment divided by the price of the property) are usually somewhere between 1% – 4%, this number is typically between 6% – 12% for office buildings (Larson, 2020).

The reason for this is simple: Businesses generate more income than families do and can allocate more resources to rental payments.

RELATIONSHIPS

As a commercial unit landlord, you won't be dealing with individuals but with companies such as LLCs. Business owners depend on their place of business for their livelihood and will thus be willing to negotiate a price that is fair and professional. You can expect them to take care of the premises because their business is also at stake.

Typically, in the case of retail outlets, you could even consider taking a cut of revenues to supplement your rental income. This is how a lot of shopping centers operate. You'll learn more about these shortly but if you own a good property on a high-traffic street, there's no reason why you can't structure a lease where you're paid a minimum payment along with a variable payment that depends on the revenues collected by the business.

In turn, the business gets to flourish and they'll maintain the property to a high standard. Keep in mind that when it comes to commercial property, you can expect your tenants to make a greater number of changes to the place. For this reason, commercial property tends to have very little frills to it.

It's usually just four walls, a floor and a roof with some doors. The tenant is allowed to make non-permanent modifications as they please. As a landlord, you will need to scrutinize these properly.

LIMITED HOURS

Businesses shut shop at the end of the day. Even the ones that work all night tend to have a reduced amount of staff working at some point during the 24-hour cycle. This means the chances of you receiving a panicked call at four in the morning are far less. Your tenants are not going to lose a key or call the cops by mistake and so on.

Commercial properties also tend to have pretty strong alarm monitoring systems installed by the tenants. If anything does go wrong, you'll have the support of the monitoring company to assist you with everything.

PRICE EVALUATION

Prior to purchasing a property, you can request to take a look at the owner's income statements since commercial owners have to maintain these legally. The data surrounding cap rates of such types of real estate are easily available and there's no guesswork as is sometimes the case with residential properties.

LEASE STRUCTURES

Commercial properties typically tend to have triple net leases. This means that all costs of maintaining the property will be borne by the tenant including taxes and maintenance, along with all utilities. This is never the case with residential leases. The reason for this is due to the fact that businesses like to maintain the look and feel of their properties and will therefore like control of the things that affect this.

Maintenance comes under the look and feel category and they'll thus take care of it themselves leaving you with less headaches.

FLEXIBILITY

Since you're dealing with a business, the government figures that they can stomach a bit more risk and will have knowledgeable people handling operations. This means there are fewer consumer protection laws applicable to commercial real estate negotiations and as a result, you can demand greater security deposit amounts and negotiate other terms of the lease, including moving out notice and so on.

DISADVANTAGES

There are some disadvantages for you to keep in mind as well. While you'll avoid the headaches that are associated with residential real estate, this doesn't mean you won't have to deal with the problems native to commercial real estate. The biggest issue will be with regards to safety issues and you will need to stay on top of maintenance issues that the lessee cannot handle.

If something does go wrong and if you're held liable, remember that an entire corporation is going to come after you and damages will be significant. All of this means that you cannot be an absentee landlord or even a DIY landlord like with residential properties. You will need to be fully licensed to carry out any maintenance on the property.

This is why every commercial property is managed by a company and these companies will charge between five to ten percent of gross rentals. This is a high price to pay but when it comes to commercial property, it's well worth it. Commercial properties can earn more rent and therefore, they tend to cost more as well.

You will need to place a bigger percentage down and the lender might not be as flexible when offering terms on the loan. There is also less governmental assistance when it comes to borrowing money for commercial purchases. Perhaps the biggest risk of them all is that your property will be open to the general public and this opens up a world of liability.

If someone slips on the floor and hurts themselves, what's the first step they're going to take? They'll sue the business. You might be found liable to a certain extent depending on the nature of the injury sustained as well as the cause of the accident. This increases the risk of investment considerably and you should take this into account prior to investing in any commercial building.

WAYS TO INVEST

You can invest in office buildings by purchasing REITs or crowd-funded REITs. The latter are often referred to as eREITs and you should study their terms and conditions carefully. Typically, REITs can be bought and sold on the open market easily but eREITs tend to have what are called lock up periods.

This means your money will need to remain parked in the investment for a certain amount of time, typically six months, before you're allowed to sell the investment. Even on selling, you might find that there are no buyers for the price you want since the trading volumes of these instruments are low.

You could also buy a building of course but this requires significant investment and as I mentioned, you'll need to put a larger amount of money down. The hospitality sector is fertile ground when it comes to investing in commercial real estate. You can try the REIT method of investment.

Alternatively, you could turn your property into a hotel-like establishment and list it on Airbnb and other holiday booking websites. You can charge higher than normal rates for this. Just make sure you don't violate any zoning laws when doing this. A non-traditional method would be to buy the stocks of hotel operators.

However, understand that by doing this you're investing in the hotel's business and not the real estate it operates. Similarly, some people buy entire hotels. This is a bet on the hotel business and not on the real estate so be careful of doing this. Typically, hotels sell for relatively cheap after a crisis of some sort. I'm mentioning this thanks to the massive hit the hospitality industry has taken thanks to the pandemic going on currently.

An interesting investment option you will sometimes see is the chance to buy hotel units. For example, you might see the Fairmont hotel selling a duplex suite or some such property. It doesn't have to be a fancy room or a hotel, you will find deals for regular rooms in regular hotels as well.

These deals are typically terrible choices for investors. First off, the fact that a hotel business needs to sell its rooms indicates that they're struggling with vacancies. Why else would the property be for sale? It's not as if the hotel is in the charity business. Secondly, you'll be at the mercy of the hotel if you want to earn any sort of rental income. The hotel acts as the property manager in this case.

When the time comes to advertise the room for travelers, you can bet that the hotel's other rooms will be filled first before yours will be. Why? Well, the hotel owns the other rooms and not yours. So why would they want to sacrifice earnings on their property by putting yours first?

Lastly, if you want to earn a cash return on the room, you will need to leave it unoccupied. After all, if you're occupying the place, how can you expect the hotel to market it as being empty? All of this is over and above the risks that the hotel business entails.

The only advantage, if it can be called that, is that you can boast that you can stay for free at the Fairmont or the Ritz. If this floats your boat, go all in by all means. Sensible investors will stay away from these kinds of deals.

SHOPPING CENTERS

While the average American mall is on its last legs, strip malls and shopping centers continue to witness high levels of foot traffic and customer demand. The reasons for this are pretty simple. Not every service can be moved online. Let's take groceries for example. People love the convenience of shopping online but for the most part, they prefer touching and feeling food products.

There are other services and businesses that require physical space to operate. Spas, restaurants and so on need retail space and shopping malls are their best bet. Given the way American zoning laws exist, the presence of a shopping center that serves a nearby community is almost always guaranteed.

Shopping centers are a part of the commercial real estate umbrella as well so let's take a look at some of the things you need to watch out for when investing in them.

LOCATION AND TRAFFIC

Location is especially important when it comes to shopping centers. This is easy enough to understand. People prefer them to be located 15 minutes away by car at the most. In addition to the shopping center's location, you should also pay special attention to the neighborhood's characteristics. Is it a safe neighborhood?

The safer a neighborhood is, the higher the rent you can charge your tenants. You'll also end up dealing with lesser liability and security issues. Lastly, your tenants will be more willing to renew their leases when the time comes. The availability of parking and entry and exit convenience is a huge factor that a lot of landlords neglect.

If your shopping center is always full then this is a good sign in the short run. In the long run though, this is a bad sign because your customers will eventually get fed up with how long it takes to shop and they'll find somewhere else to go. Preparing and budgeting for a parking space expansion should figure in your plans at some point.

Measuring the vehicle traffic in front of your shopping center is also important. As a rule of thumb, most shopping center investors aim for vehicle traffic of 50,000 per day. The local county traffic department might have statistics on this. If this fails, you might have to spend a day with a clicker. This might seem extreme but some landlords go so far as to measure even foot traffic into their shopping center.

Lastly, take a look at the current tenant mix and check whether this matches up with the demographics of the neighborhood. The local chamber of commerce will have statistics based on the recent census data that you can refer to. Ensuring the right mix of tenants to match demographic demand is essential for success.

AGE

If you're buying an existing center, you must take note of how old the property is. The older the property is, the higher your maintenance bills will be. You might even have to refurbish the place to make it suitable for new tenants. Age is also a leverage point when it comes to negotiating a price.

You can strike a deal with the seller that has them replace any problematic areas in the property prior to purchase. This will reduce your ongoing bills and will relieve you of any headaches for the short term. Just make sure the repairs and maintenance being carried out are adequate and not superficial.

TENANT QUALITY

A lot of landlords get their tenant mix wrong and end up souring relations with the local community. National chains and anchor stores offer higher rents and landlords automatically opt for this thereby ignoring smaller local businesses in the process. You must have an even split between national chains and local businesses, assuming there are enough high-quality local businesses that want to rent space.

Local businesses will create a natural draw to your center since this is what builds community relationships. Having said that, you need to be realistic about the bottom line as well. Take a look at rent rolls and past payment records of existing tenants. Speak to the owners personally.

Often you can choose to lower their rents for a lower fixed payment and add a variable component that is a percentage of their revenues.

This makes you invested in the success of their business and a lot of business owners will appreciate this.

LEASES

Commercial leases are more complex than residential ones. The former usually contain a number of caveats and floating renewal and commencement dates. These dates are typically contingent on repairs and maintenance being carried out or on some payment being made (*What To Look For When Buying Shopping Centers*, 2020).

Carefully review these leases and create a calendar of renewal and commencement dates to get a picture of the cash flow characteristics of the property.

Hiring the help of an attorney is a good thing to do since many clauses tend to be quite complex for the average investor to figure out.

COMPETITION

Generally speaking, it's a good idea to avoid competition. At the most, if there's another shopping center nearby then this is a sustainable level of competition. A lot depends on the size of your property and the size of the population being served as well. There are no easy metrics to determine this but the average foot traffic and rent levels in these areas will help you figure out where the competition is too much.

This is because very few customers are going to be loyal to a shopping center outlet. At most, you can expect your anchor tenant, usually a supermarket, to inspire loyalty. However, customers will usually flock to the places that offer the cheapest prices and discounts. This means your tenants will not be able to afford high rental payments. This means less profit for you.

Too much competition simply leads to a race to the bottom and no one is going to win that. If you spot high levels of turnover and month to month leases in your shopping center, then this is a bad sign and it means that tenants come and go quite often. Eventually, they'll stop coming because business isn't sustainable, and this will make your investment a terrible one as you can imagine.

Shopping centers are also susceptible to new projects being built in their catchment zone. A catchment zone refers to the size of the community your center serves. This is why it's essential to have a healthy number of local businesses in your property. This will keep people coming back to you even as the national chains open competing stores in a new center.

REITS

Shopping centers are an expensive investment so a lot of investors will be better served buying into mall REITs. Despite the word 'mall' in it, these REITs invest in shopping centers since the average mall is on its last legs in this country.

The capital appreciation of these REITs tends to be a bit more volatile and tracks the property rates around the country. You must also pay attention to all of the points that I've highlighted just now when evaluating a REIT. While calculating traffic and so on might be impractical since the REIT likely owns hundreds of properties, you should pay special attention to the consistency of their income and payments.

Take note of the depreciation expense as well. Depreciation is an accounting expense that is applied to older assets. Their values are reduced as time goes on. In the case of a REIT, the asset is the real estate property itself. Older malls require constant maintenance and if you notice that depreciation expenses are getting lower, this means that the property portfolio is quite old.

Why lower and not higher? Well, older properties will be written off as time progresses. The newer the portfolio is, the higher depreciation expense will be since all properties need to be depreciated. In contrast, if a REIT has an 80% allocation in older properties, most of these will likely have been fully depreciated already and thus, the expense will be low.

All in all, shopping centers can be a great investment but you must perform thorough analysis of the property in question. Beginners are best served by investing in REITs since these make analysis pretty straightforward. All you need to do is take a look at the company financials to figure out what's going on. This is not always the case with a physical property.

RAW LAND

There are many types of raw land you can invest in. Perhaps the most lucrative of these is the purchase of farmland or timberland. Generally speaking, raw land purchases have a lot going for it. The thing that attracts people to this asset class the most is that land is scarce. After all, the world's population is growing, and it isn't as if we're reclaiming tons of land from the sea.

This means that land prices automatically increase every year. It's not as if they increase by large amounts but they do steadily go up over time and follow a completely different cycle from the stock market and residential/commercial real estate. This makes raw land investments a good hedge against market moves.

Typically, cash yields from raw land investments are low. On average, an investor in American farmland earns a yield of 3.3% per year. This can be boosted by converting raw land into farmland but even here, investors can expect yields of around 5% which is lower than what brick and mortar residential real estate offers.

The primary attraction here is the security aspect of the investment and steady capital appreciation. This is especially true when investing in timberland. Typically, this land requires plantation of trees and it can take up to five or even ten years for the trees to mature before their wood can be harvested.

Mulberry trees tend to mature within five to six years and are a sustainable source for making furniture. They're always in demand and the investor will earn a decent amount of cash flow from their purchase. However, the flip side is that they need to wait a while before this happens.

Farmland investing can be a lucrative way to invest. The problem is that sourcing high quality farmland is difficult. This is because the majority of farmland in the United States is owned by farmers. Currently, close to 60% of harvestable farmland is farmer owned (DiLallo, 2020).

This leaves 40% for you to buy. You might think this is a lot but corporations tend to snap this land up pretty quickly and in huge chunks which leaves around two to three percent for smaller investors. There's a reason this land is being left behind and you'll be hard pressed to find a great deal.

The best way to approach this is to purchase land that has an existing tenant. This way, you can be sure that the land is producing something and that you aren't being sold a marsh in disguise. A more sustainable way of investing is to join your competition.

If you cannot compete against bigger companies, join them! The bigger companies that are buying land are REITs and you can invest in them through the stock market. These REITs invest across a multitude of farming classes. You'll be able to gain exposure to commodity farming (soybean, livestock, corn), food crops, organic farming, fruit and vegetable farming and even vineyards.

Raw land investing can offer many benefits. As long as you educate yourself with regards to the characteristics of the specific investment opportunity you're looking at, you'll be fine.

NON-TRADITIONAL INVESTMENTS

In addition to the categories mentioned thus far, it is possible to invest in non-traditional real estate assets such as data centers, industrial structures and warehouses. There are no rules of thumb with regards to investing in there. Truth be told, the average investor is best off avoiding them because of the complications they can bring.

If you happen to be particularly knowledgeable about any one of them, then invest in them by all means. You can also invest in REITs that specialize in such investments.

CHAPTER 4
REAL ESTATE VERSUS STOCKS

The stock market forms a handy benchmark against which all investments can be evaluated. Real estate returns are often evaluated against the returns of the S&P 500 both in terms of quantity as well as in terms of volatility. Volatility is often looked at as being on the riskiest factors of stock market investment.

Real estate prices don't fluctuate on a daily basis as much as stocks do. Besides, there's also the fact that capital appreciation is the primary profit driver of most stocks. While REITs and a few stocks do pay dividends, their yields are a lot lower than that of physical real estate.

So, when it comes down to it, which is the better option? Many investors have differing views so let's take a look at the differences and relative advantages of each option.

INVESTMENT CHARACTERISTICS

Both types of investments behave in different ways. After all, investing in physical real estate involves buying an actual brick and mortar property and this comes with its own requirements. Stock market investing meanwhile requires a different set of skills and it's a lot easier to make mistakes with this.

STOCK INVESTMENTS

The first thing to note about stock market investing is that you can buy stocks in companies that are attached to the real estate market or you can buy instruments like REITs that offer you direct exposure. For example, you can buy stock in companies that build homes or stock in real estate development companies and so on.

These can be lucrative investments, but you must keep in mind that the real estate market is not the only thing that determines the profitability of such companies. While this is the primary driver behind the company's growth, there's also the matter of evaluating how competent company management is at identifying key growth drivers and opportunities.

Incompetent management can sink a company in a profitable business pretty quickly. A great real estate market will not save it. Another example of these kinds of investments is to buy ETFs that are linked to soybean and corn prices. Investors typically choose these instead of investing in raw land that produces these products.

This is a mistake more often than not. While the raw land purchase will give you a cut of the profits from the sales of the crop, this doesn't mean that purchasing the commodities will give you the same exposure. Commodity prices are affected by a lot more than the conditions prevalent in a small piece of land. There are broad based economic factors to consider as well.

Then there's the fact that as an investor you won't actually own any soybean or the physical commodity. You'll instead own the futures contract linked to it. Futures are complicated financial instruments and it's best for beginners to stay away from them as much as possible.

These kinds of indirect investments in real estate are usually not a great idea because you'll introduce a bunch of external factors that will determine the success or failure of your investment. Instead, it's far better to invest in a REIT where you'll be directly earning the rental income on the property, through the REIT.

The thing to note here is that you won't have actual ownership of the underlying property but will instead own a piece of the management company (the REIT). This entitles you to a cut of the profits and this is what you'll receive. REITs have expenses to account for so typically, there will be a mismatch between the property's rental yield and the distribution you receive.

For example, the underlying properties might be yielding six percent, but you'll receive distributions of three percent. This is because the REIT pays out 90% of its net free cash flow and not the rental income. The rental income is the only source of revenue for the REIT and it uses this money to pay for operational expenses.

It's important to keep this distinction in mind. When you look at the underlying portfolio of the REIT, don't look at just the rental yield and think that's what you'll receive. Crowdfunded real estate has been on the rise of late and these offer investors the opportunity to get in on some good deals.

As of this writing, crowdfunded real estate does not offer great investment value to most investors. This is because they're less tradable than regular REITs and also have lock up periods when you cannot withdraw your money. Regular REITs have none of these flaws so sticking to normal REITs is a better bet.

The great thing about owning a REIT is that you'll automatically diversify your risk. The REIT will own a mixture of properties and with a single purchase, you'll be able to gain exposure to a large variety of property. This ensures that your cash flow is not going to be overly dependent on the fortunes of a single property. In other words, if a single tenant leaves, you've still got a large number of properties providing you with income.

PHYSICAL PROPERTY INVESTING

Investing in physical real estate has its own characteristics. The most obvious characteristics of this kind of investment is that you'll be the owner of the property. If conditions demand it, you are fully entitled to move into the place and live in it and there's nothing anyone can do. This provides people with a great measure of security. After all, there is a place you can always return to in case you need it.

Physical property ownership also gives you an advantage in that you can access funds on the basis of your equity in the property. This opens up further avenues of investment. For example, you could borrow money against the existing equity in your home and use that to finance the purchase of another property, thereby increasing the size of your portfolio and cash flow.

The value of your property is linked to the local real estate market's trends and also the national market. While the national market plays some role, it is the local demand and supply that affects it the most. This doesn't mean your property's value doesn't depend on broad market moves. It's just that major national occurrences will influence its value.

For example, changes in the interest rate will affect your home's value but it's not as if you'll see huge swings in prices. However, if local demand dries up, you'll see a huge change in the valuation of your home. This makes the behavior of physical real estate different from investing in REITs.

REITs are sensitive to national level changes (unless they happen to be locally concentrated REITs) thanks to the large portfolio of properties they own. Thus, the capital appreciation of your investment is linked to the overall stock market trend and economic conditions to a greater degree.

With a physical investment, you will often see that your county or state will remain unaffected by national events. This offers advantages and disadvantages which you'll learn about next.

PROS AND CONS OF PHYSICAL REAL ESTATE

Both categories of investments offer their own advantages and disadvantages. It's important to keep in mind that neither category of investment is inherently good or bad. Their suitability for you depends on your own viewpoints and preferences. For example, some people do not want to deal with the hassles that physical ownership brings. Such people prefer investing in REITs instead.

Take the time to understand both sides of the coin before making a decision. With this being said, let's look at the advantages of physical real estate.

ADVANTAGES

The first advantage of owning brick and mortar real estate is that you have direct control over the property. Even if you choose to delegate its management to another entity, you have full control over it and have the final say over what goes on with it. For example, if you wish to remodel your property to change its appeal to renters, you're free to do so.

A common example of this is when landlords decide to remodel a large two-bedroom property into a three or four bed property. If you find that demand is arriving mostly from college-aged people, then creating smaller bedrooms from larger ones will allow you to earn more money from the property.

These advantages are obviously not present when it comes to investing in REITs. With a REIT, you're pretty much delegating the management and allocation of your money to a management company and you have no say over such matters. This highlights a bigger advantage that physical property ownership gives you.

You're in full control of the asset's present and future and can respond accordingly to changing demographics. Investors often change the curb appeal of their properties to make them more attractive to renters or carry out new installations and upgrades to allow them to earn more rent. There are many ways you can force capital appreciation with your property, and these are just a couple of examples.

You also have flexibility in deciding what sort of a tenant you wish to attract. As long as you're abiding by fair housing law practices, you're free to decide what sort of a renter you wish to let to. If you find that pets are particularly problematic for you, you're free to not allow pets on your property. If you wish to convert the property to appeal to seniors, then making it more accessible is entirely in your control.

This allows you to explore more paths to greater income which you cannot do with a REIT. You're pretty much stuck with the income profile of the investment you bought and are dependent on the managers entirely. Then there's the fact that a physical real estate investment is just easier to understand.

After all, you can touch and feel the property. You can ask yourself whether you would like to live there. Would you like to live in the neighborhood if you had kids, or if you were in college or if you had a particularly fussy dog and so on. You can get into the shoes of your renters (your income source) a lot easier and make decisions.

The cash flow is also easy to understand. You have expenses every month and earn rent. The difference between the two is your profit and free cash flow. That's all there is to it. You don't need to dissect an income or cash flow statement to be able to make a decision on the viability of the investment. This ease of understanding will enable you to make better decisions with regards to your investment.

You'll also be able to source better bargains with physical real estate. Remember that the local real estate market moves to its own rhythm as compared to the national one. You could spot situations where someone is going through a tough period and their property is being foreclosed on despite the market being a great one.

This means that you can source a great bargain here and can earn huge yields. There are also a number of resources to help you find great properties that offer great value. Websites such as Roofstock and Zillow have a large number of listings that will allow you to carry out a great amount of research from the comfort of your home so it isn't as if you need to pound the pavement looking for opportunities.

While REITs typically yield around three percent, it isn't uncommon for a real estate investor to earn a rental yield of above six percent. A lot depends on the property being invested in of course, but with the right level of due diligence, you can source some great deals. Best of all, you'll be in full control of the type of tenant you want to attract and can increase the yield by carrying out some improvements.

One of the biggest advantages of physical real estate investment is the tax advantages it provides. Landlords can write off a number of expenses as tax deductions and these come in handy during tax time. The expenses of running a rental property ultimately turn out to be a lot lower than expected as a result.

The other function of property as I've already mentioned is as a shelter of funds. Property prices remain relatively stable and aren't as volatile as stock market prices. Besides, there's the added security of there being something physical present as an asset. This leads to a lot of wealthy people buying real estate as a means of preserving their wealth and avoiding expenses such as inflation.

Outside the United States, many governments offer significant incentives to get people to buy real estate. Some European countries offer so-called golden passports where a purchase of property above a certain monetary value gives you the right to permanently reside in that country or become a citizen.

All in all, physical real estate has a number of benefits that investors can take advantage of as you can see.

DISADVANTAGES

With the good comes the bad and for all of the advantages that physical real estate offers, there are a few disadvantages as well. While all of these can be mitigated by adopting certain investment methods and simple preparation, the fact is that the existence of these negatives will make physical real estate unsuitable for some people.

The first disadvantage is the sheer size of the investment. Entering the investment requires capital upfront in the form of the down payment and closing costs. This typically runs into the low five figures and even this amount can be up to 20% of the overall cost of the property.

A lot of people will be deterred by such a high cost of entry. Then there's the fact that in order to generate wealth, you'll need to borrow money. There's simply no other way to generate wealth rapidly via physical real estate because of the price tag of the investment. Having this much capital locked into a single investment is problematic for a lot of people.

You need to plan it years in advance and will need to double check everything to make sure you're doing things the right way. This isn't a negative as such but it does require you to dedicate a significant amount of time to figure all of this out.

If you happen to make a bad choice or just run into some bad luck, then you're pretty much stuck with the property. After all, selling a home is not as easy as selling your stock holdings. In the stock market all you need to do is click a button and that's it. When it comes to selling a home, it'll take you months if not a year to receive a serious offer.

The entire time your home is on the market, its perceived value decreases as does your bargaining power. If you happen to have really terrible luck and run into a recession, then a bad investment has the ability to wipe you out completely. This is what happened to millions of Americans between 2007 and 2010 when they discovered that their homes were worth less than the value of the mortgage.

It's not as if the banks will let you off because of this. You'll still owe the higher mortgage payment and if you fail to pay, you'll face the prospect of a foreclosure which effectively bars you from borrowing money for a period of at least two years. All in all, the effect of illiquidity of physical real estate is very real and this is why preparation is essential.

One of the things that causes such problems is poor lender practices. Typically, lenders don't carry the mortgage on their books and instead sell them onto larger corporations. This means the lender's sole incentive is to issue as many mortgages as possible. This doesn't mean they'll give everyone a free ticket, but it does cause bad practices in marginal cases.

The problem with this is that the borrower is ultimately the one that pays. They might initially think that they've scored a good deal by paying just five percent down instead of 20% and receiving a floating interest rate that is many points below prevailing rates. However, they fail to realize that all of these promotional terms come to an end at some point and when the real rates kick in, they'll be deep underwater.

Excessive leverage causes foreclosures even when the buyer has prepared well in advance. For example, unforeseen circumstances such as job loss or an accident might put significant strain on the financial situation and will cause people to miss payments. Leverage cuts both ways ultimately. It allows people to own expensive assets for little upfront but it also hits back way harder if things go wrong and makes the situation a lot worse.

Even when things go well, physical rental properties need active management. Land-lording is close to a full time job if you buy a multi-unit property. There's always something that needs fixing or maintenance. You cannot be an absentee landlord unless you want to outsource the task to a management company. This will usually cost you around four to five percent of the rental income every month.

This might seem like a good tradeoff, but it opens you to the risk of hiring a bad manager. If that company doesn't do its job well, you're the one that suffers. Essentially, you'll move on from managing the property to managing the manager. Either way, it's going to cost you time.

Successful real estate investment requires some knowledge of the local real estate market and a bit of financial savvy in understanding how financing works. There are more advanced strategies that employ complex financing options. Now, you won't have to learn all of this right now but if you want to concentrate on real estate investing, you'll need to figure these out.

Beginners are best served by networking in their area and meeting more experienced real estate investors through clubs or on websites such as Facebook and LinkedIn. Networking allows you to get to know the market well and see if your numbers make sense. Success comes down to running the numbers well and in this regard, the stock market does offer easier opportunities.

Speaking on the stock market, it's pretty easy to spread your capital across multiple investments when you invest in stocks. Different asset classes are readily available for you to invest in and in fact you can gain exposure to multiple asset classes by purchasing just one instrument such as an index fund or ETF.

This is impossible in physical real estate. You're completely dependent on the local economy and market and have to hope that everything goes well. You might find yourself in a situation where things are bad locally but nationally, this isn't the case. In such scenarios, diversification helps a lot but given the high leverage and high cost of entry, this isn't entirely possible.

PROS AND CONS OF INVESTING IN STOCKS

It's pretty easy to gain exposure to the stock market. All you have to do is open an account with a broker and click the buy button. This is also a major disadvantage since you're likely to indulge in your worst behavioral traits by doing this. Let's take a look at the advantages and disadvantages of investing in the stock market.

For purposes of simplicity and comparison, I'm going to stick to looking at the traits of property investment related securities and not the entire world of the stock market.

ADVANTAGES

Liquidity and the ease of buying and selling is perhaps the biggest advantage that the stock market offers. If you're invested in a REIT, you can buy exposure to millions of dollars worth of rental income at the click of a button. You can also sell that exposure back to the market just as quickly. Physically, this would be impossible.

REITs also allow you to choose your level of diversification easily. If you like investing in hospital related property, then you're free to purchase a hospital REIT. If mortgage financing is your thing then you can buy a mortgage REIT that issues mortgages to property developers.

If you want exposure to the broad real estate market, then you can purchase a diversified REIT that holds a little bit of everything. It isn't just REITs, you can do the same if you're buying companies related to real estate. If you want to purchase stock in a home builder's company or a landscaping service provider and so on, you can do so to whatever extent you wish. Of course, you can also invest beyond real estate just as easily with stocks.

Most people start off with the stock market because the barrier of entry is low. You can invest either a lump sum or invest small amounts of capital over a long period of time. Some investments do have minimums, but these are laughable compared to the required upfront payments in real estate.

Investment minimums usually amount to $3,000 unless it happens to be a fancy hedge fund type of investment. Given that hedge funds are not available to regular folk, you'll never have to worry about these minimums. A stock market investment is you effectively giving the managers of the company control of your capital.

You're allowing them to make decisions on your behalf as best as they see fit. This means you're free to go about doing whatever you want and don't need to worry about the state of the toilets in the underlying properties. You're not going to be called to manage the property at any point and all you need to do is sit back and collect dividends.

Income collection is a great feature and the best part is that all of this income is completely passive. All you have to do is invest money and the rest takes care of itself. This is impossible in physical real estate as you've seen. The catch is that yields are lower. However, for some people, the lack of activity might provide adequate compensation since it frees up their time to do other things.

DISADVANTAGES

A lack of control is what turns off a lot of prospective investors. One of the biggest advantages of physical real estate investment is that it gives you full control over the state of your property and all decisions related to it. When it comes to stock investments, your only decision is to buy or sell. This doesn't make much sense to some people when they're investing in real estate.

After all, what's the point of property ownership if you cannot use it as you please? This indirect ownership structure doesn't give you any claims on the asset. In fact, you own a piece of the management company and not the property itself. If active ownership appeals to you, then a stock market investment is not the right choice.

If physical real estate requires you to have knowledge of the local market, investment in a REIT requires you to understand the market that the REIT has exposure to. For example, you could be living in North Dakota and invest in a REIT that manages office buildings in Philly. How well do you know that environment? This makes your investment risky since you're completely at the mercy of the REIT's managers.

The prices of the REIT will fluctuate on a daily basis with a lot more volatility than their underlying assets. Stock market prices move for a variety of reasons and understanding which reasons are valid and which ones are invalid is a tough task. You could end up ignoring some very valid developments or act on insignificant ones. This might cause you to cash out of your investment far too soon and forego all the gains you could have earned.

Finally, stock market investments don't offer anywhere close to the tax saving benefits that physical real estate does. They're simpler to prepare but the flip side is that they don't really save you money.

At the end of the day, you can clearly see that the pros and cons of both types of investments cancel on another out. Choosing which one is better for you is a question of asking yourself which disadvantages are you comfortable living with. Running the numbers properly is the key to making your investments work, no matter which choice you pick.

CHAPTER 5
GET YOUR HANDS DIRTY

At this point, you've learned all about the basics of real estate investment and now, it's time to take a look at some strategies you can employ in the market. These strategies are related to physical real estate investment.

By the end of this chapter, you'll not only understand the different methods you can implement but also how each strategy works, and which one might be best suited for you based on its characteristics.

STRATEGY #1 – PLAIN VANILLA RENTAL PROPERTY

This is the most straightforward and common method of property investment. The basis of it is pretty simple. You buy a property and rent it out thereby collecting rental cash flow as well as capital appreciation over the long term. A property that is ready to be placed to rent immediately after purchase is called a turnkey property.

In some cases, you might find that there are existing tenants living there. This is great because it means that your cash flow will begin from the first day. There are many steps for you to take prior to earning that cash flow so let's look at them in order.

PROPERTY TYPE

The first thing for you to do is to review what sort of a property you wish to invest in. There are different types you need to take into consideration as you've already learned. Beginners are best off investing in residential real estate since there is a vast support network for these types of property.

Commercial property has its own rhythms and can be profitable however you'll likely be dealing with seasoned investors and this might put you at a disadvantage. Furthermore, financing is tougher and hinges on your prior experience. Remember that there will be activity connected to your investment after your purchase goes through and you cannot expect 100% passivity with it.

Once you've decided on what type of property to look for, your next step is to figure out where you want to invest.

WHERE TO INVEST

This is a huge step and good preparation here will ultimately determine your success with your investment. This is also where the one percent rule will be applied first. Many people choose to invest in their own backyard or zip code but remember that this should not be an automatic choice.

While investing close by provides convenience, it might not be the best bargain for you. Investors tend to do this because of emotional attachment to their neighborhoods and tend to overestimate their knowledge of where they live. You might know everyone's names around you but this hardly means property in the area is a good investment!

At a basic level, you want to look for properties in neighborhoods that meet the following criteria:
- Demand for rentals is high
- Supply is low and vacancy rates are low
- Economic expansion and job growth are growing or steady
- The one percent rule is satisfied. At this stage you'll have estimates but the rule will help you quickly figure out whether a property is a good investment or not.

- You can afford the average price of property. If the average price is $200,000 and you're looking to pay $10,000 down, you cannot afford this place. This is because traditional lenders will want you to pay at least 20% of the property as a down payment. Closing costs are typically up to five percent of the purchase price.

Once these factors are satisfied, you'll need to drill down some more and take a look at the micro trends in the neighborhood. Some key statistics to pay attention to are:
- Prospect of future developments that will affect supply and demand
- Crime rate
- Presence of schools
- Average property values
- Average rental values
- The trends for both
- Presence of specialize rentals such as student housing, senior living or pet friendly communities. You can either avoid or target these as per your choice.

There are some resources that you can use to gather all of this information. Mashvisor is a website that provides data on rental prices and the potential viability of the investment in an area. A paid site that offers a ton of data is Local Market Monitor. This website offers all data from rental yields to cap rates to demographic statistics.

Department of Numbers is another website that provides all kinds of economic statistics for free as does census.gov. The latter is run by the U.S government and you'll find the latest demographic data for a zip code on the website. Keep in mind that you'll still need to visit the property and cannot expect the numbers from these sources to replace the need to physically look at the neighborhood.

Another trick you can use to determine the exact numbers is to search for the websites of local realtors. These websites will sometimes have data directly from the MLS. MLS stands for multiple listing service and this network has the most up to date information and price histories of properties around the country.

Realtors and real estate professionals are the ones who typically have paid access to this network due to the fact that they use this data to prepare comparisons prior to putting together an offer. While large websites such as realtor.com and Zillow have listings, these are typically not from the MLS and the data can be varied.

In order to drive more traffic to their websites, smaller agents typically list this feed on their websites, and you can benefit from this.

FINDING PROPERTIES

Once you've fixed your criteria, it's time to begin searching for your property. You have multiple options when it comes to this. There are the bigger websites that I've just mentioned or you can work with a realtor familiar with the neighborhood. A realtor is a great source of information and will also have a network of professionals whose services you will eventually need such as lawyers, contractors and so on.

Keep in mind that the realtor's objective is to sell the property since this is how they'll earn their profits. This puts their objective at a slight conflict with yours and you'll likely find that some realtors will push you towards properties that might not be a good fit for you. Therefore, while it's great to work with them, keep in mind that you want to make your own decisions and do your homework.

A good way to evaluate a realtor is to ask them questions about the area and demographics and match their answers to your research. Watch for inconsistencies in the way they respond to your queries and how frank they are about the market. Real estate agents sometimes specialize in certain types of properties.

Some might specialize in vacation rentals (you'll learn about this later in this chapter) while some support flippers (the next strategy you'll learn about). When it comes to plain vanilla rentals you want to look for agents who specialize in turnkey properties. Be warned that these properties don't always offer the best deals in terms of price appreciation.

This is because their conditions happen to be pristine and they will have existing tenants in them. They'll also need no remodeling and will be marketed to you as being a passive investment. Some of these properties will even have a property management company handling all of the rent collection and other landlord duties.

Therefore, all you need to do is collect cash on your investment. This is how a lot of turnkey properties work and they are great passive investments. However, keep in mind that should things go south, you will have to step in yourself. They're also not the most efficient of investments since you'll be paying for the convenience of doing nothing.

If you want to get your hands dirty with land-lording, turnkey properties are not your best choice. However, if you want the least number of headaches and are prepared to pay for it, this is the best investment option for you.

RUNNING NUMBERS

This is the core of your strategy and is what will make things work for you. Your objective here is to figure out the net cash flow of the property. This is the rental income minus all the expenses you will incur with the property. You'll also need to calculate the cap rate which is the net income divided by the purchase price.

Lastly, there's the cash on cash return. This measures your yearly return on the amount of cash you've invested. Let's run through these numbers by running through an example. Let's say you've located a property worth $200,000 and your down payment requirement is $40,000. Closing costs will be 4% of the purchase price so these work out to $8,000. Thus, your cash investment is $48,000 and you'll be financing $160,000 via a mortgage.

At this point, I'll need to make some assumptions about your financial situation. First off, I'm going to assume that you have good credit with a FICO score between 620 and 719. Next, here are the additional assumptions I'll be making:

Interest rate = 3.8%

Term of the loan = 30 years

Conventional loan and not an FHA or VA loan

Property adheres to 1% rule

All of these inputs are necessary to calculate your monthly mortgage payment. This works out to $745.53. You can use the calculator at https://www.mortgagecalculator.org/ to estimate this number.

Next, you need to estimate the costs of running and maintaining your property. As you've already read, the 50% rule is a great way to estimate this. Since the property adheres to the 1% rule, we know that the rental amount will be:

Estimated rental amount per month = 1% of purchase price = $2,000 per month

Cost of maintenance and running expenses per month = 50% of rental amount = $1,000 per month

In this example, I'm assuming that you're investing in a turnkey property. This means you won't have any rehab costs but you will have to pay a management company 10% of your rental revenue per month. So, let's now look at what your net profit looks like:

Rental revenue = $2,000

Costs = $1,000

Management cost = 10% of rent = $200

Net operating income = $800 per month

Cap rate = Annual net operating income/ Property value = (12*800)/200000 = 4.8%

However, from a cash flow perspective for an investor, this really isn't worth it. Now, with the above calculation, I have erred on the side of caution. I've included management expenses over and above the 50% expense rule. Typically, the 50% rule includes all management fees.

Another point to note is that the calculation of net operating income above does not include the mortgage expense. This is because you should use the operating income calculated to figure out if you can really afford to borrow the amount of principal you intend to.

As you can see the operating income is $800 per month which is slightly higher than the mortgage payment of $745.43. In other words, you're going to be paid to own the property which is a great thing! In real life, you'll probably see a negative cash flow but keep in mind that you're building equity in an asset and are gaining in terms of capital appreciation.

At this point, you can play around with the principal you wish to borrow to see how you can boost your cash flow per month. For example, using the previously highlighted calculator, let's assume that we want a positive cash flow of $200 per month.

This means we want out mortgage payment to land somewhere around $600. This means you can borrow around $130,000, maintaining the same assumptions we previously made. At this point, you have a choice to make: Should you invest more cash upfront ($30,000 more) to earn a positive cash flow of $200 or should you borrow that amount and reduce your monthly cash flow to a negligible amount?

Your cash on cash return will be: Yearly net operating income / Cash invested = 9600/28000 = 34%

It comes down to what your exit strategy is. Most real estate investors look to exit by refinancing the property and withdrawing their initial cash. This is also called a cash out refinance in lending circles. The way it works is that you build equity in your property and once you reach a certain level of ownership, you refinance your mortgage.

Let's say you borrowed $160,000 from our example above. You begin with 20% equity in the property. After a while, let's say you reach 40% equity (you own $80,000 with the remaining $120,000 owned by the bank). At this point, you can refinance by applying for a new mortgage for $120,000 and receive a check for the amount you wish to withdraw.

Let's say you invested $30,000 initially and want to withdraw this amount. You'll apply for a new loan that will be worth $150,000 ($120,000 of what you already owe plus $30,000 that you want to cash out). You'll receive a check for $30,000 and your home equity is adjusted accordingly. You'll continue to make mortgage payments according to your new payment schedule.

This method is used by a lot of real estate investors since it allows them to realize a 100% cash return and then use that cash to invest in another property. Alternatively, you could hang onto the property or simply sell it down the road. You'll receive a check for the percentage equivalent of the equity you own in this case with the bank taking the rest.

In other words, if you own 40% equity in the home at the time of sale and manage to sell the property for $250,000, you'll receive $100,000 and the bank will pocket $150,000. This is the recommended method of exiting from a rental investment for beginners. Cash out refinance has its own pros and cons and you'll need to have a good level of experience to pull it off.

Generally speaking, it works best when you have multiple properties. For now, just focus on running the numbers properly and focusing on how much you want or can stomach as a cash inflow or outflow per month.

STRATEGY #2 – FIX AND FLIP

Fixing and flipping is what most beginners to real estate associate with investing in real estate. The idea behind it is very simple. You find a property that is in a state of disrepair, make the repairs and sell it back onto the market. Sounds simple, but executing it is quite difficult.

The most difficult part of the flipping process, and there are many difficult bits, is obtaining financing. Most lenders will not lend to flippers. What's more, most buyers will also not qualify for a mortgage on your property. The reason has to do with an old rule that the Federal Housing Authority (FHA) used to impose.

Under this rule, any property that was previously sold within a 90-day window of being offered once again onto the market does not qualify for an FHA loan. Therefore, if the buyer loves your property, they'll not be able to obtain the financing necessary to purchase it and you'll be stuck with it. FHA borrowers are a sizable portion of the market, so this isn't all that great for you.

Having said that, there are ways to make flipping work but you'll need to keep a sharp eye on the numbers. The process begins in the same way as the previous method. You scout for listings and network with other investors to locate properties. When it comes to flipping, some of the best deals come from real estate wholesalers.

Wholesaling is a bit of a gray area in real estate but many people practice it anyway. Wholesalers tend to be experts in the local market but don't have the cash to put down on deals. As a result, they spot properties that are potential flips and approach investors with the idea of earning a cut of the proceeds.

The way this works is this: The wholesaler will sign the original purchase contract but will then assign it to you for a higher price. The difference in prices is their profit. Alternatively, you could approach a realtor for such properties. Again, keep in mind that a realtor would love to offload a terrible property onto you since that's what their aim is.

I'm not saying they'll stick you with a terrible property on purpose. It's just that they have their own business to worry about.

OFFER PRICE

A good rule of thumb to apply here is the 70% rule. This states that your offer price should not be more than 70% of the estimated after repair value of the property minus repair costs (Davis, 2019). For example, if you're looking at a property worth $100,000 and its after repair value (ARV) is $130,000 and you'll need to spend $10,000 repairing it, your offer price should not be more than:

Offer price = (130000-10000) * 0.7 = $84,000

The lower you can go the better. Keep in mind that if the seller is willing to accept a ridiculously low price, you're probably coming off worse in the deal. So your risk on the deal isn't just about the numbers alone. Keep seller motivation in mind as well.

FINANCING

Unless you have the cash lying around, you're going to need to finance the purchase. This is where it gets tricky. Traditional lenders will not lend to you although a few small banks will. This is because they need the business. A more conventional route flippers take is to approach hard money lenders.

These lenders offer higher interest rates and will require greater down payments on their loan. However, they will lend to you and if the numbers you've worked out are correct, you stand to make a significant profit. Given that the timeline of these projects tends to be around six months at the most, you'll find that the high interest rates are justified given the profit potential.

The flip side is that if things go wrong, you'll have significant running costs. In other words, if you fix it but can't flip it in time, you'll need to assume high interest payments on a place you have no intention of living in.

WHAT TO LOOK FOR

As tempting as it may be to do otherwise, it's best to scale into the business by first purchasing a property that needs minimal repairs. This way you'll have a better handle over repair costs and can even carry them out yourself. Fixing and flipping is not a passive investment strategy so expect to be involved with the project from start to finish.

Some investors turn their properties into plain vanilla rentals and refinance the property to reduce interest burden. This way they earn higher capital appreciation as well as the rental income. The critical part of this strategy is estimating repair costs.

A good method is to build a margin of safety every step of the way and place a 10-15% buffer on every expense estimated. You will also need the help of an experienced contractor that can help you with these costs. Prior to getting into flipping, it's useful to connect with a few people in the business and speak to them about how they work and what you can expect in terms of timelines.

Keep in mind that even the contractor is estimating costs and they won't know for sure until they actually begin working on the project. This is why placing a buffer on costs is a good idea. A key thing to keep in mind is that you should discuss all terms of the contract with your contractor. What is the scope of the work to be carried out? How will they handle any increase in scope?

A key thing to discuss is the disposal of waste. Repairs often produce a ton of waste and a high-quality contractor will dispose of it in a responsible manner. Examining the way they leave the workspace at the end of the day is also a key marker of efficiency. If you see tools strewn about or work left half done, this is a bad sign.

In terms of access, you need to discuss how this will be handled. If the repairs are small enough you could let them in at the start of the day and lock up at the end of it. If the scope of the work is large, then it makes sense to give them a key as well. Make sure you change the locks once work is complete.

When it comes to rehab do not take on any remodeling projects or additions. This is because these don't add as much value as you think they might and even worse, in some states you will need a building permit to carry out such work. All of this costs you money and time and they profit you receive just isn't worth it.

CALCULATING PROFIT

The numbers work the same way as they do in plain vanilla rentals. It's just that in a fix and flip you'll have the additional cost of rehabbing the property prior to selling it or renting it. Using the same numbers as before, let's look at how we can structure our deal.

The property is currently selling for $200,000 and you'll have to put 20% down and the closing costs are at 4% as previously. Your ARV is estimated at $275,000 and your estimated repair costs are $15,000. This means, a safe offer price using the 70% rule will be:

Offer price = 0.7* ARV – rehab costs = $177,500

Down payment = $35,500

Closing costs = $7,100

The thing to keep in mind is that if you're going to be placing this property for rent after you fix it, you want to keep the 1% rule in mind. In this case, as long as you can get $1,775 as rent per month, you'll make money on the cash flow.

Calculating the NOI and the cash on cash return is exactly the same as before. If you manage to sell the property within your chosen timeframe then your return will be:

Total profit = Cash received – Cash invested = (20% of ARV) – (down payment + closing costs + rehab cost) = (275000*0.2) – (35500+7100+15000) = ($2600)

As you can see, this deal results in a loss. Keep in mind that this is just a back of the envelope calculation. Once you begin to get into the actual work you'll find that expenses will be a lot higher and that your ARV values might not reach the levels you want them to.

I'd like to point out that you'll receive 20% of the ARV because that is the equity you'll have in the property if you flip it. You paid

20% down and your equity is going to remain pretty much the same over a short period of time.

One way of boosting profit is to reduce the cost of repairs. Generally speaking, the more expensive the property is, the higher will the cost of repairs be. This is simply because buyers will expect a higher standard of living with such homes. By rehabbing a lower priced home, you'll dramatically lower costs since you can get away with making simple cosmetic changes that buyers will accept.

A good example of this is to simply repaint the existing cabinets and storage instead of installing new ones. Painting them white is a hack that many flippers use since this gives them a new look and best of all, it's cheap.

The above example required $15,000 in repairs on a $200,000 home (that would be sold for $275,000). If you lowered your sights a bit and instead purchased a property worth $80,000 that could be sold at an ARV of $110,000, the property's appreciation is a lot less but you will end up making money if the repairs are a lot less. Here's how the numbers would work in this scenario:

Offer price = $54,000

Total profit = cash received − cash paid = (110000*.2) − (10800 − 2160 − 4000) = $5,040

Cash on cash return = Total profit/ Cash paid = 29%

As you can see, a lot depends on the discount you receive on the list price as well as the expected ARV. Both play an important role in the eventual profit you'll make.

STRATEGY #3 – VACATION RENTAL PROPERTY

This strategy is an offshoot of plain vanilla rentals but here you'll face a far higher turnover of tenants thanks to the nature of the property. Typically, investors purchase such properties in vacation hotspots and as a result, the rental income is either seasonal or it faces a high turnover of tenants.

To be honest, this strategy works best when the investor is seeking to shelter their wealth and the rental income is a preferred add-on at best. Such properties tend to be expensive and they usually will not conform to the one percent rule, unless you manage to score a great deal.

The properties themselves tend to be prestige properties. What I mean is that the investor can boast of owning such a property but in terms of income production, their potential is low. When it comes to implementing such a strategy, it's best to first check to see whether alternative methods of investment are not a good option.

For example, wealth advisors recommend their clients purchase a second home once they have enough exposure to the stock market and bonds. The aim here is to diversify the investor's money and it really isn't to earn rental income. Typically, these investors hire a property manager to list the homes on platforms such as booking.com or Airbnb.

This means that the rental yields over a short term tend to be high but over the long term, they even out thanks to vacancy rates being high as well. When it comes to non turnkey plain vanilla rental investing, landlords usually estimate a 10% vacancy rate. In other words, they estimate that their properties will lie vacant for around one to two months at the most in a year.

With vacation rentals, you'll often see vacancy rates closer to 70% in seasonal areas and 50% in destination with year long appeal. This is because competition will be a lot higher in the latter areas and the additional presence of hotels will cut into your vacancies.

As a wealth generator, this isn't the best strategy. Most purchases are completed in cash since the objective is to preserve it. You can use this property as a second home, in which case your rental income will be reduced. However, that's not the point to begin with so it's unlikely to hurt you.

All in all, vacation rentals offer opportunities but truth be told, the property investor isn't the one who witnesses the most profit. It is the management company that earns the most since they can easily build a portfolio of properties quickly and reduce their per unit service costs.

Over time, their profit per unit increases and this is how the business grows. The savvy investor might consider investing in such a company instead of a property if it suits their risk profile.

STRATEGY #4 – FORECLOSURE INVESTING

Foreclosure investors tend to combine the properties of plain vanilla investing and flippers into one. This is because buying foreclosures and other bank-owned properties gives them deep bargains in terms of offer price and often these properties have been abandoned and left to rot.

The real trick to making foreclosures work is to have an efficient system that will ensure you get the best deals. A good place to start is on bank websites. For example, Bank of America lists a number of properties that it has foreclosed on and investors can bid on.

Their website lists the name and contact details of the agent and you can easily get in touch.

Companies such as Fannie Mae and Freddie Mac that buy mortgages from lenders have a steady stream of listing on their websites. During bad times, these listings explode in size as you can imagine. Another good way to source deals is to find a good agent who specializes in foreclosures.

As I mentioned earlier, agents tend to specialize in certain types of deals. A foreclosure agent will be able to source HUD listings of homes for you. HUD stands for the Department of Housing and Urban Development and they list a large number of foreclosures on their website at hud.gov. The downside of HUD homes is that there is no room for negotiation.

You have to take the place as is and you're responsible for all repairs. County officials also have weekly auctions for foreclosed homes. Many counties have websites where the listings are posted and they'll place a public notice as to the date of the auction. Another option is to pay foreclosure listing services a fee to bring you the best deals.

These range from $50 per month to $200. It all depends on the kinds of deals they bring. Lastly, keep in mind that all of these methods are inferior to having a trusted agent whom you have a good relationship with. Often, agents will be able to bring you deals that haven't hit the market as yet.

In terms of numbers, they're exactly the same as in the plain vanilla and flipping cases. Foreclosed homes will typically need some sort of repair before they're inhabitable. If your agent is able to bring you a deal before the home is foreclosed, you might be able to score a great deal without the need to conduct repairs.

Keep in mind that you're dealing with sellers who are desperate and have had something go terribly wrong in their lives. While this is a potentially great situation for you, they're well aware of why you're present. So while your aim should be to get a good price, don't run away with yourself and offer something that's demeaning because you feel they're desperate.

At the end of the day, it can be tough to find great deals due to the amount of competition you'll face. The best way to source them is to develop a network and to move quickly when one appears. Often, the best deals are sourced from your network. So spread the word at your local investment club and with the local agents in your area.

A particular hurdle that most investors have is the high cost of investment. Typically, such deals tend to be 70% cash financed and as a result you will need to have substantial cash resources to make it work. The other thing to keep in mind is that you will need to have a good network amongst hard money lenders to be able to secure financing for such deals.

This concludes our look at investment strategies that you can implement in physical real estate. All of them have varied objectives but the numbers you need to look at and the way the math works with all of them are pretty much the same. At the end of the day, do your due diligence and always keep the cash in versus cash out equation in your mind.

CHAPTER 6
INVEST FROM YOUR COUCH

As I've mentioned earlier, physical real estate isn't the only way for you to get a slice of the real estate pie. You can invest in the market through stock instruments. Keep in mind that this doesn't count as direct ownership but given the relatively low entry hurdles, the stock market is a great way for investors to diversify into real estate.

The primary driver behind such real estate investment is the REIT. Let's take a look at this first.

REIT

I've mentioned previously how REITs are essentially companies that manage large properties and pass their earnings onto their shareholders. This is because of the way they're structured. You see, REITs are mandated by the government to pass 90% of their net income to their investors.

Why would any company agree to do this? Well, the simple answer is that they get benefits. In the case of a REIT, this comes as zero corporate taxes. Thus, many property management companies convert their structure to a REIT and end up saving more money.

When investing in REITs you should be careful to distinguish between the rents that that company collects and the dividends they distribute to their shareholders. There are two forms of income a REIT can earn. The first, and primary method, is rental income. The second is via a sale of assets.

For example if a REIT owns a shopping mall and they wish to sell it for whatever reason, the capital gains on that sale count as earnings. REITs are full-fledged companies and have expenses such as office rents, salaries and so on. Thus, these costs are subtracted from revenues and 90% of this number is paid to shareholders.

Therefore, any analysis of a REIT involves looking at the company's financial statements and this can make things complicated in a hurry. With this in mind, I'll first present an easy way you can invest in REITs without having to worry about analyzing statements. For those who are interested in taking it further and getting into the details of the business, I'll present a way to analyze the finances of the company afterwards.

THE EASY WAY

The stock market presents a lot of risk to investors and the prospect of losing your capital is ever present. The truth is that there is no way to predict how a business will perform in the future. The best thing you can do is hazard a guess. To mitigate this risk, a particular method of investing was developed back in the late 80s.

The name of this method is called index investing and to understand this, we need to look at what an index is in the first place. An index is a collection of stocks that fulfill certain criteria. For example, the S&P 500 is an index that contains the 500 biggest stocks in America.

Big in this context refers to the market capitalization of the company. This is calculated by multiplying the share price by the number of shares outstanding. Practically anyone can create an index. Even you! If you wish, you can create an index of stocks whose names begin with 'X' and follow their fortunes.

The popularity of the index depends on the authority that created it. This is probably why an index created by S&P or Dow Jones will have more of a following than the one you created. As you can imagine, REITs have their own indices all of which have their own criteria.

For example, the FTSE Nareit All REITs is an index that tracks every single REIT that trades in the United States. Here are some of the others that you can find:
- MSCI U.S Reit Index – Similar to the FTSE Nareit
- FNCO – FTSE Nareit Composite index – Tracks the biggest mortgage and equity REITs.
- FNER – FTSE Nareit equity REITs – All equity REITs
- FN15 – FTSE Nareit office REITs – All REITs invested in office buildings
- FN20 – FTSE Nareit retail REITs – All REITs invested in the retail sector such as malls and shopping centers.

These are just a few that exist currently. The great thing about indices is that they're designed to capture the best performing stocks according to the criteria that's applied. For example, let's say you decide to take a look at FNCO. This tracks only the biggest REITs, whether they're mortgage or equity, in the U.S. If a certain company falls foul of the criteria of the index, it is automatically dropped.

The value of the index is a composite of the value of its individual parts. Thus, since only the best performing stocks tend to remain in the index, the index's value itself rises over time. Over a long period of time, the value of the index has to rise since inflation along with economic growth will ensure that there will always be companies that replace poorly performing ones.

Take the S&P 500 for instance. Back in the 1970's a significant chunk of this index was dominated by industrial stocks. These days, technology dominates the index. Despite the nature of the economy changing, the S&P still managed to rise over this time period because it simply kept adding the best stocks and dropping the poor ones.

You might be thinking that this is great. All you need to do now is buy the index. Well, that's the bad news. You can't buy indices. Instead, what you can do is buy index funds or exchange traded funds or ETFs.

Index funds, as the name suggests, simply follow an index. Their managers buy shares in the stocks in the index and rebalance it as the index changes. This means they capture the performance of the index, whether it increases or decreases. ETFs can have any number of strategies but there are a large number of them that follow index investing strategies and simply follow an index.

This has great advantages for the investor. For starters, all they need to do is buy a fund (a single purchase) and instantly, they've diversified their holdings into all of the stocks in the index. What's more, they don't need to worry about what their money will do over the long term since the index will replace itself with the best stocks over a long period. Sure, it will decrease and drop over short-term timeframes but the overall trend is upwards.

The best part is that the index fund collects the dividends paid by the underlying REITs and passes them onto you. In return, you pay a small management fee which is usually less than 0.1% of gains. Thus, the income is fully passive, and you get to keep all of the benefits of investing in a REIT. Best of all, you've secured yourself from a steep drop in the value of a single REIT.

After all, companies come and go, who knows which company will be present tomorrow? However, the index removes this risk since if a company does drop out, another takes its place and the index moves forward. The downside to this is that you cannot expect outsized returns. You'll capture the average.

However, keep in mind that you have to do nothing except buy the fund and that's pretty much it. For those who want a more active strategy and can stomach greater risk, you will need to be able to analyze financial statements. Let's look at the relevant metrics you need to understand.

ANALYZING FINANCIALS

When it comes to REIT analysis, the two financial statements you need to pay special attention to are the balance sheet and the cash flow statement. All companies that trade on the stock exchanges have to file an annual report with the Securities and Exchange Commission (SEC).

The SEC stipulates that three financial statements that detail the company's performance need to be filed. These are the balance sheet, income statement and the cash flow statement. The balance sheet lists all of the assets and liabilities the company has. The income statement details the revenues and the costs associated with the business and the cash flow statements details the cash flow from operations, investment, and financing.

So why is the income statement a bit deceptive when it comes to REITs? Well, truth be told the income statement is slightly deceptive to begin with. This is because income does not equal cash in the bank. Companies are complicated things and often they will need to book revenues before cash hits the bank.

For example, let's say you need to pay rent for your apartment but instead of paying monthly, your landlord asks you to deposit one check that covers the entire year. If your lease begins in January, this means that the month of January will see you paying a huge amount of expense while the remaining months will see lower expenses.

If you were to report these numbers as is, it doesn't present an accurate picture of your living expenses does it? Now imagine if this same scenario occurs over the course of a few years. This is what companies undergo. They have expenses that hit all at once in a particular year that will reduce their profits significantly if they report it as is.

In order to present a more accurate picture, they smooth these expenses and revenues out to present a clear picture. A key component of the income statement is the depreciation expense. Let's say a company buys furniture. This is an asset and gets recorded on the balance sheet at the value for which it was purchased.

However, the value of this furniture is not going to remain the same throughout. As the years go by, its value decreases. How much does it decrease by though? The only way to know this is to offer to sell it and see what buyers are willing to pay. This isn't a practical way of conducting business as you can imagine.

What accountants do instead is reduce the value of these assets over a period of time at a certain rate per year. For example, furniture might be depreciated at 10% per year. If it was worth $100 at purchase, it's worth $90 a year after and $80 a year after that and so on.

The thing with real estate is that assets appreciate over time. A well-maintained property increases in value after all. Yet, the SEC mandates that property must be depreciated. A REITs primary asset is property and this leads to a bizarre situation where assets keep shrinking while rental payments increase thanks to capital appreciation.

Thus, the cash flow statement, which adds depreciation expense back to income is far more relevant. After all, depreciation is not a cash expense. The company does not witness a cash outflow because its furniture decreased in value from $100 to $90. Cash flow measures the amount of cash that came in, what went out and what the net cash was.

This is termed the free cash flow. Your task is to look at the trend of the free cash flow and to see whether the company can continue to realistically keep paying out dividends from this amount. The way to look at it is to pay attention to the capital expenditures and the quality of assets the company is carrying.

Is management saying the right things about growth and are they reading conditions well? How do they plan on reinvesting the profits the company makes? All of these things can be gleaned from the annual report. Your task is to look at these statements and see whether the free cash flow backs this up.

There will be tough years in between and the company will make losses. However, the manner in which management handles these tough times is important to look at. Many investors look just at the dividend yield and use that as a metric. The yield is the dividend payment amount divided by the share price.

Some investors make statements that say that they only invest in REITs that yield greater than five percent. This is a nonsensical statement to make. Historically, REITs have yielded three percent which is double the yield of stocks. A REIT can have high yields but keep in mind that a high yield can be caused by a falling stock price as well.

So don't look at just yields. Instead begin by narrowing down your preferred area of investment. Do you want a diversified REIT, or do you want to concentrate on shopping center REITs or hospital REITs? Do you want to invest in financial REITs? These REITs provide mortgage financing to projects and don't own any property themselves.

They do carry out some complex financial engineering but if you're able to understand this, then invest in them by all means. All in all, REITs tend to be highly diversified and they are easily traded. This means you're not going to find yourself in too much trouble if you wish to sell your REIT at market prices.

Their lower barriers of entry and the fact that you can earn a dividend from the income of the REIT make them a great investment.

TAXATION

REIT taxation is a bit complex on the surface but it's quite straightforward once you understand the concepts inherent within it. REITs pay two types of dividends. One portion of the dividend is called the ordinary dividend and the rest is called return of capital or ROC.

The dividend comes out of the free cash flow so how does the REIT decide what is ordinary and what is ROC? Well, the IRS does this for them. IRS rules state that the portion of dividend that is greater than the reported earnings (on the income statement) is the ROC portion. Anything up to the reported earnings is the ordinary portion.

Ordinary dividends are taxed at your marginal income tax rate. ROC is a bit different. The taxes on this are deferred to when you sell your investment in the REIT. These are taxed as capital gains which can be either zero, 10, 15 or 20% depending on your income tax bracket.

However, the key thing to understand is that if you never sell the REIT, you never have to pay these capital gains taxes. You can simply pass them on to your kids and the effective cost of purchase is adjusted to the price they inherited the investments at. They can thus continue to enjoy the benefits of the free ROC until they sell their investment.

This is a huge advantage that REITs transfer to their shareholders and this isn't present in regular stocks.

INVESTING IN REAL ESTATE SECTOR STOCKS

If REITs don't catch your fancy for whatever reason, you can choose to invest in companies that operate in real estate. For example, you could build a portfolio that contains the stocks of the biggest developers, the biggest financing organizations and lenders.

Keep in mind that this is an indirect way of investing in real estate and in reality, you're investing in a company that is connected to the market less directly than a REIT is. You're exposing yourself to the vagaries of the company's business. For example, real estate developers routinely face cash crunches and their business cycles are independent of the overall real estate market.

In other words, the market might be booming but if the developer cannot organize cash in time to pay their banks, the boom isn't going to do much for them. You can buy a sector via an index fund or ETF to diversify your risk. However, keep in mind that there is a danger of you moving away from real estate investment into something else.

CHAPTER 7
KEY RULES OF THUMB

Real estate investing can be made even more powerful and successful if you follow some simple rules of thumb. This way, you'll save yourself a lot of time and money and will be able to quickly evaluate the potential profit of a deal.

This chapter is going to walk you through some key rules of thumb, six to be precise, that will let you know whether an investment is worth it or not.

THE ONE PERCENT RULE

This was the first rule that was introduced to you and it is also the most powerful one. The rule itself is brilliant in that it quickly allows you to calculate whether a deal is worth it or not. Having said that, there are some disadvantages to it that I'll detail later in this section.

For now, let's look at why it works so well. By requiring your properties to produce rental income per month that is one percent of the purchase price, what you're effectively saying is that you're looking for rental yields of 12%. This is a huge yield and is something that every investor will be pleased with!

However, remember that we haven't taken costs into account as yet and these will decrease your overall yield. Furthermore, costs have a nasty habit of being unexpected. Ensuring a 12% yield on your investment right off that bat gives you a good buffer to be able to accommodate these surprises.

Let's look at an example to see the power of this. Let's say you see a home that is listed for $100,000 and your aim to establish this as a rental property. Given the one percent rule, you need to generate at least $1,000 per month in rentals from this property for it to be worth your while.

Let's say you estimate costs to be half of this rental amount but then you suddenly encounter a huge problem that requires you to spend a greater amount of cash to fix the issue. So how much of a buffer do you have? Well, you can spend up to 100% more per month above your current expense level.

Your costs are $500 per month and this gives you a buffer of $500. Thus, you immediately know how much of an additional expense you can stomach. Having such a large buffer also helps you build a margin of safety into your investment. A margin of safety is just a way by which investors can account for the unexpected.

While the one percent rule is great, it can create some drawbacks.

DRAWBACKS

The biggest drawback is that in real life, finding such great deals is a bit unrealistic, especially for turnkey properties. Even the ones that you will find will have some kind of catch or undetected repair to it. Thus, while the rule is excellent, you will need to dig further to rustle up some deals.

The biggest disadvantage for the long term is that you might end up missing out on some great opportunities. The one percent rule doesn't take into account the fact that a few cosmetic changes to the property can create huge capital appreciation. For example, giving the building a fresh coat of paint and fixing the landscaping alone will allow you to generate more rent.

Also, the fresh look that the building receives will help you realize a gain in the value of the property because its curbside appeal will increase. There are properties that don't adhere to the one percent rule but still provide huge gains that make up for it. If you were strict about this rule, you might miss out on these deals.

With that being said, the rule is still a great way to guesstimate your returns and the probability of a deal being worth your while. As you become more experienced, you'll find that you'll apply more discretion when it comes to this rule and you'll begin to screen deals where you can realize appreciation in other ways.

THE 50% RULE

While the one percent rule is aimed at the profit side of things, the 50% rule saves you from losing money and firing a torpedo at yourself. In short, it's more important than the previous rule when you're starting out. People are notoriously bad at predicting things and our ability to estimate them gets worse the less experienced we are.

A key part of your success is your ability to estimate your costs and run the numbers on your deal. Beginners to real estate investing tend to look at the rental income and subtract the cost of utilities and maintenance and leave it at that. Maintenance is an estimate so the way they do this is ask themselves what a pipe would cost to fix and simply extrapolate that number over the course of the year.

They don't take into account a lot of other things that could go wrong and that costs them money. For example, even the most optimistic landlord in the world would never assume that their property is going to be occupied all the time. It's going to be empty at some point and this will cost you money.

It won't cost you cash, but it'll hurt your bottom line nonetheless in terms of reduced cash flow. Then there's the expense of management. You might think that you'll simply manage the property yourself but keep in mind that your time is worth something. If you work at a job that pays you $85,000 per year, you're effectively earning $40 per hour if you work eight-hour days.

Now imagine spending three hours every day maintaining your property that detracts from your time spent at work. In effect, your property is costing you $120 every day. This is again a non-cash expense but it is a very real one. This is why some investors prefer to delegate property management to companies.

If the rent you're earning from our previous example is $1,000 then the management company will charge $100 per month as fees. You're better off spending $100 and making $120 during those hours instead of losing $120 managing the place yourself. That's a perfect example of being penny wise but pound foolish.

The 50% rule brings all of this together into a simple formula. Everyone can divide by two and this quickly allows you to estimate how much you need to pay as expenses from your rent. It smooths out all of those intermittent charges and gives you a simple calculation to deal with.

THE 70% RULE

The 70% rule as explained in the section in flipping property is a powerful one when it comes to ensuring you'll earn a decent return for your efforts. The rule is particularly powerful because it builds a margin of safety into your calculations right from the start and it also enables you to move quickly and produce an offer price.

The rule itself is quite straightforward. Your offer price on a property you're looking to fix and flip should be 70% of the ARV less the costs of the rehab. ARV stands for after repair value and this is the price at which the property will sell once repairs are completed. Estimating this value can be a bit tricky but there are ways to arrive at a proper value.

The first person to check with is your agent. Keep in mind that the agent's objective here is to sell the place and they're not going to be shy about boosting the price. I don't mean to say that they'll tell you something worth $100,000 is $500,000 but you can expect some exaggeration. A good way to double check their claims is to ask for a record of recent sales in the area.

This will give you a good indication of prevailing trends. In addition to this, the agent will have access to the MLS, and they'll be able to tell you how long the property stayed on the market on average. This is also helpful for you because you'll get an idea of how long the sale will take once you're done fixing the place.

There are no guarantees that your plan will go through on schedule and this is why you need a margin of safety. In addition to this, building a 10-15% buffer in the rehab costs is a good move as well. This way, you're protected from any unforeseen circumstances related to repair work.

Applying the rule is just a question of doing some simple math. If the ARV of the home is estimated to be $120,000 and your repair costs are $12,000 then your offer price should be $72,000. This seems like a great deal but keep in mind that you need this buffer to allow for all costs related to the flip.

As you become more experienced, you'll find that higher end properties don't necessarily need to be approached in this manner. This is because the dollar value of the ARV will be higher to begin with and you'll have more wiggle room in terms of the type of rehab you wish to carry out. While the rehab will cost more, there are lots of cosmetic fixes you can carry out that buyers will be happy with.

For beginners, this is a great rule since it removes all guesswork and the need to itemize costs.

CAP RATES

The cap rate is your return on the property's price. Investors often get confused between cap rates and the cash on cash return. These two values will be the same if you pay for the property in cash. However, if you paid via financing then your cash invested in the deal is limited to the down payment and closing costs and the two values will differ.

Cap rates are calculated by dividing the net operating income of the property by the total value of the investment. The net operating income in turn is calculated by subtracting the cost of maintenance and running the place from the rent payments. The 50% rule comes in handy when calculating cap rates.

Many investors wonder what a good cap rate is. The answer is that it depends. Let's say you're in an area where property prices are high. Cap rates will naturally be lower in such places since the higher the property's price is, the lower the cap rates will be.

Your agent will be a good source of cap rate information in the area. Resist the temptation to fix a certain number in your mind and go after that number no matter what. This is one of the mistakes that beginner investors make. They read about someone making seven to eight percent cap rates and think that that's what they should be making when the market will not support more than three or four.

Do your research and see if the local cap rate makes sense. Calculate your cash on cash return. Remember that this is the net operating income divided by your cash investment in the case of a rental. In case you sell the property, this will be your profit divided by the cash investment you made when purchasing the place.

Looking at the cash on cash return is a good way to determine the viability of the investment. Cap rates are useful when it comes to determining whether you're generating the right levels of income from the property. For example, if your cap rate is 5% but the average rate in the area is 7%, your expenses are either too high or you're just not charging enough rent.

Cap rates keep changing as per real estate cycles and you'll find that they'll increase during downturns. This isn't because the operating incomes have increased but it's due to the fact that property values have decreased. So keep in mind that there are two parts to the equation.

DIVIDEND YIELDS

Just like how people get fixated on certain cap rates, they can get fixated on earning certain dividend yields. The dividend yield is the distribution paid by the stock divided by the price of the stock. If you buy something worth $50 and it pays you $1, the yield is two percent.

Given that dividend yields are a stock market subject, there is a lot of emotionally charged talk about what is a good dividend yield. Some people claim that an investment that doesn't yield 5% is not a good one. Let's look at how much sense this makes. Suppose we have two REITs A and B. REIT A is a diversified REIT that has stable revenues and is yielding 2%.

REIT B is more volatile due to its high concentration in mall investments. Not shopping centers but malls. It's yielding a spectacular 10%. However, its price has declined from $50 to $20 in that time and its yield has gone from 4% to 10% during this period. In other words, when it was priced at $50, the dividend payment amount was $2.

At its current price, it's paying 10% of its price which means the payment amount is $1. The bottom line is that the dividend payment has decreased 100%, the price has decreased 60% but the yield has increased by 4%. If you were to blindly purchase the higher yielding REIT, B would be the one you would buy.

But is this an intelligent thing to do? It's clearly facing bad business prospects and has cut its dividend. In what world does B make a better investment than A? Greed often drives investors towards REITs such as B. They look just at the yields and neglect everything else to do with the business.

This is why you need to begin by determining what sort of exposure you'd like. Do you want a diversified REIT or do you want to get into something more concentrated? The more concentrated you get, the higher your payouts can be but you'll also be exposed to more risk when things go bad. Yields are an imperfect measurement and should never be your primary concern when it comes to investing.

The only scenario where it makes sense to invest in the higher yield is when you have two similar investments, both of which are stable, and you can't decide which one to invest in. In this case, go for the higher yield since this makes sense.

All of these rules of thumb are dirty guesstimates and you should not rely on them to produce exact numbers. Their function is to give you a quick picture of whether an investment is a good idea or not. They aren't meant to replace your ability to calculate the numbers in detail.

As you become more experienced, you'll find that these rules won't always apply. However, when starting out, it's best to take note of them and use them to your advantage.

CHAPTER 8
SHOULD I QUIT MY JOB?

A common question that eventually occurs to real estate investors is whether they need to quit their job or not. Real estate investing can be a full-time job and truth be told, it's a bit difficult when you start out. Most people hold full-time jobs and find land-lording or coordinating a fix and flip difficult.

Perhaps the biggest constraint occurs when you're trying to locate suitable properties. This chapter is going to guide you through those first few months and also give you pointers on when you can seriously consider quitting your job and going full time with your investments.

THE EARLY DAYS

Before you get into investing in real estate, you must keep in mind that it's going to put a strain on your time. To be frank, fixing and flipping is an extremely tough strategy to pull off when you have a full-time job. This is because you're competing against full time investors with access to the MLS. These people typically tend to be licensed agents as well and as a result, their costs are lower.

They also have the ability to produce an offer within a few hours and negotiate deals within a day. If you're stuck at work, there's no way you'll be able to access such deals even if you set up alerts or ask your agent to notify you immediately. With this being said, it's not as if you can't pull it off.

You can develop a good relationship with your agent and notify them as to what you're looking for exactly. If you feel confident that the agent knows your preferences and understands your financial needs, then empowering them to make an offer immediately might work. However, most beginners aren't in such a position.

This is why focusing on foreclosures or plain vanilla renting is the best option for such people. This way, you'll be facing less competition, especially with turnkey rental investing, and you'll manage to get your foot in the door and begin building equity. There are some preliminary steps you need to take to make sure that your time is being spent wisely.

NETWORK

You need an active roster of agents and contractors on your contact list. These people should be doing the leg work during the day, looking at deals and thinking of you when they come across an opportunity. If you're looking at a foreclosure that needs some work, you need to be able to have your contractor take a quick look at the place and give you a decent estimate of repairs needed.

Often, your agent will bring you pre-foreclosure properties. These tend to move quickly, and you'll need to be on your toes. While the agent can spot these properties, it's up to you to make a move and meet with the owners and produce an offer. This can be a bit challenging so take a look at your work schedule and see if you can make it work for you.

You might need to drop everything and drive over to the seller to figure out what's going on. A lot of full-time workers cannot afford to do this so it might not be for you. When it comes to plain vanilla rentals, you should still have your contractor or an expert take a look at the place to see if any repair work is needed.

Understand that contractors are busy people and they're not going to drop everything and drive to some place just to take a look. You can't keep asking them for favors and not give them some business at the end of the day. So be careful with how far you push it. Lean on the agent as much as you can since they have a monetary stake in the transaction.

Have your agent leverage their network of real estate professionals such as attorneys and title companies so that your time is spent effectively. It might be tough but with some proper planning prior to investment, you can make this work easily for you.

FINANCIAL PREP

Before investing in real estate, you need to make sure that you have at least five to six months' worth of expenses saved up as hard cash. Keep in mind that these are not just living expenses but also expenses that the property will bring. If your property doesn't rent within your planned time frame, can you bear the additional mortgage payment?

Many investors don't factor this into their expenses. They count on the rent to reduce the mortgage payment, but they forget that the property can lie vacant for a while or there might be an economic downturn. Leverage kills such people's finances and they'll eventually find themselves facing a foreclosure.

WHEN TO QUIT

The decision to quit is a lot easier than people think. You can consider quitting your job when the income you earn from your investment fully replaces your salary and you have six months' worth of expenses stored away. Keep in mind that depending on your strategy, your income from real estate might be intermittent but it might average to a steady number.

For example, flippers often find that their incomes vary with the number of deals they find. In cases where incomes are uncertain, you'll need to figure out what suits you best. Most people find it hard to live with the up and down nature of their income and if you happen to be one of these people, you could consider turning your rehab into a rental investment.

Generating positive cash flow is the objective here. In the beginning, this is tough to generate. You might find that you'll need to refinance and buy a property for cash in order to drop the dependence on financing so that you can earn all of the cash flow from your property. This takes time and careful planning.

Don't put a timeline on it and instead work your way towards building a decent portfolio of three or four properties. Once you're at this point, you can consider refinance options or even a sale to boost your cash levels and invest in deals that can generate positive cash flow.

Patience is the key to success in real estate and as badly as you want freedom from your job, keep in mind that this takes time and careful planning.

CONCLUSION

Real estate investing can be intimidating to a beginner but with careful planning and by utilizing the proper strategies, you can achieve financial freedom. It all begins with understanding the basics of real estate investing and by understanding the different types of property you can invest in.

Keep in mind that while physical real estate requires a high upfront payment, you can invest in the stock market and produce some real returns. This is done by investing in REITs and these instruments don't cost much more than the average, common stock. REITs tend to pay a large dividend but do not fall into the trap of chasing yields blindly since this will lead you to ignore the underlying fundamentals of the investment.

Fundamentals are the key in physical real estate investments as well. You need to figure out the cash flow characteristics of the investment and make sure that the cap rate and your cash on cash returns make sense. While the rates might be high, don't neglect the financing part of the equation. You will need to balance your returns with the mortgage payments.

In most markets you will find that the mortgage will be higher than the net operating income. However, this is not a bad thing since you'll be owning the property and the capital appreciation will make up for it. Besides, once you've built enough equity in your home, you can refinance it and cash out or reduce your mortgage payment rates.

There are some handy rules of thumb you can use to determine the viability of an investment. With plain vanilla rentals the 1% rule and the 50% rule come in handy. With fix and flips, the 70% rule will help you figure out the correct offer price.

All strategies require varying degrees of work to succeed and you need to prepare ahead of time to figure out how you can build a support team that will do the work for you as much as possible. It will be tough at first but over time you'll find that you'll be in a position to quit your job and achieve your dream of financial freedom!

I wish you all the luck and wealth in your real estate investment journey. This book has given you a great head start on the competition but now, it's up to you to go out there and implement everything you've learned.

Do let me know what you think of this book and how it's helped you in the field of real estate investing. Once again, good luck with your real estate investments!

REFERENCES

Average Rent in Manhattan & Rent Prices by Neighborhood. (2020). https://www.rentcafe.com/average-rent-market-trends/us/ny/manhattan/

Brumer-Smith, L. (2020). *Top 5 tax advantages of real estate investing.* https://www.fool.com/millionacres/taxes/real-estate-tax-deductions/top-5-tax-advantages-real-estate-investing

Carson, C., Luis, K., & Olivier, BJ. (2019, October 28). *What you didn't know about appreciation in real estate.* https://richonmoney.com/appreciation-in-real-estate/

Davis, B. (2019). *What is the 70% rule in house flipping?* LendingHome Blog. https://www.lendinghome.com/blog/what-is-70-rule-in-house-flipping/

Davis, B. (2020). *Real estate vs. stocks: Which performed better over 145 years?* https://www.biggerpockets.com/blog/real-estate-vs-stocks-performance

DiLallo, M. (2020). *Investing in farmland: A real estate investor's guide.* https://www.fool.com/millionacres/real-estate-investing/investing-farmland-real-estate-investors-guide/

Larson, M. (2020). *Pros and cons of investing in commercial real estate.* https://www.nolo.com/legal-encyclopedia/pros-cons-investing-commercial-real-estate.html

Library Guides: Prices and Wages by Decade: 1960-1969. (2020). https://libraryguides.missouri.edu/pricesandwages/1960-1969

United States Initial Jobless Claims 2021-2022 Forecast. (2020). https://tradingeconomics.com/united-states/jobless-claims

What To Look For When Buying Shopping Centers. (2020). https://www.raisal.com/blog/buying-shopping-centers-multi-tenant-retail-investment-properties/